NATIVE AMERIC.
ART PROJECTS

Susan Major-Tingey

SCHOLASTIC
PROFESSIONAL BOOKS

New York • Toronto • London • Auckland • Sydney

Cover and interior design by Frank Maiocco
Art Direction by Vincent Ceci
Cover photograph by Donnelly Marks
Interior photographs by Susan Major-Tingey, Donnelly Marks, Jaime Lucero
Interior illustrations by Scott Russell

ISBN # 0-590-25635-1
Copyright © 1995 by Susan Major-Tingey
All rights reserved.
Printed in the U.S.A.

12 11 10 9 8 7 6 5 4 3 2 1   1 2 3 4 5 6 / 9

CONTENTS

CALIFORNIA/GREAT BASIN/PLATEAU

NORTHWEST COAST

ARCTIC

MESO AMERICA/ CENTRAL AMERICA/ SOUTH AMERICA

INTRODUCTION

The purpose of this book is twofold: to provide a means of introducing students to the wide array of American Indian artistic traditions and to present a variety of projects that can be adapted for any group and setting, regardless of the age of the students involved or the time and resources available.

It has been impossible here to cover the entire breadth of Native American art. The styles and techniques invented and developed by Indian artists are just too numerous to cover exhaustively in one volume. In pre-Columbian North America alone, there were more than 350 Indian tribes—each of which had its own unique lifeway, worldview, and type of artwork. Understandably, I have not attempted to include examples from every Indian group or of every native art style. Instead, through careful selection, I have tried to develop lessons that as a whole provide a sense of the diversity of the artistic creations made by the Indians of the Americas, both past and present.

STUDYING NATIVE AMERICANS

When studying the art and artifacts of Native Americans, it is important to address how and why these objects were originally created and used. To help provide some cultural and historical context for these projects, I have included in each lesson a brief description of the role played by the object in the Indian society that produced it.

In these descriptions, I have also tried as much as possible to note when and under what circumstances Indians were making a particular type of art. Once non-Indians began arriving in the Americas in large numbers, the world of most Indian peoples was in constant flux. The rapid changes they experienced and the sometimes amazing adaptability Indians showed in response were reflected directly in their artwork. Therefore, I have frequently noted how non-Indian materials, techniques, and designs affected traditional art forms—sometimes for the better, sometimes for the worse. Sharing this information with students will help them understand the enormous creativity of Indian artists and also counter the stereotype of Indians as "backward" peoples frozen in time.

HOW THIS BOOK IS ORGANIZED

The projects here are organized geographically by what anthropologists refer to as culture areas. The Indian groups in each of these areas shared a similar way of life, in large part based on their immediate environment. This organization highlights another important theme to pass along to your students—how greatly the region in which a tribe lived dictated almost everything about their society and culture, including the artworks they produced. On the most basic level, Indian artists' natural surroundings had a profound effect on their work because it determined the raw materials they had at their disposal. But just as important, it also influenced how much time they had to devote to their art. For instance, the Indians of the Northwest Coast were prolific artists in part because of the region's mild climate and abundance of food sources. Surviving in such a rich environment took little effort; therefore, they could afford to put their energy and time into making art.

In the titles for each lesson, I have identified the project with one Indian tribe or group, either because these people were masters of the art form or technique described or because one of their artisans produced the work on which the project was based. However, in general, the art and dwellings made by different Indian peoples living in the same culture area were fairly similar.

HOW THESE PROJECTS WERE DEVELOPED

In developing these projects, I had different aims with different lessons. Some are intended to familiarize students with a type of art object made by Native Americans. Others explore an art technique or type of pattern or design associated with a certain Indian group. Still others provide instructions for creating copies of specific works, in many cases pieces made by contemporary Indian artists. (Be sure to let students know that these projects were inspired by modern works as a way of impressing upon them that the arts remain a vital part of Indian life today.)

Despite their various goals, these lessons have other qualities in common. They all have been used effectively in a number of classroom situations. Their instructions are easy to follow, so a teacher does not have to have any special art training to present this material well. In fact, the directions are simple enough that students who can read should be able to follow them and, in many instances, make the projects without supervision.

For some lessons, I have offered several methods for producing the same project. My intention was to provide teachers with enough choices that they can easily adapt any project to suit their classroom. For all of the lessons, I encourage you to further customize the materials and methods used to fit your own circumstances.

BUDGETING YOUR TIME AND MONEY

Knowing the limited budgets of many classrooms, I also have tried to suggest materials that most schools have on hand or that can be collected without too much effort. Nevertheless, I urge you not to ignore an activity just because it calls for materials you cannot afford. Feel free to simplify a project in order to eliminate a costly material or to substitute different supplies. (Keep in mind, for instance, that nearly every project in this book can be made with paper.)

Remember, too, that careful planning can help you make the most of the supplies that you do have available. Many of these projects use the same or similar materials. Doing several such lessons will allow you make use of materials left over from one project on the next.

MAKING THE PROJECTS WORK FOR YOU

The lessons here have been tested successfully with students from kindergarten through eighth grade. Obviously, the simplest activities are most appropriate for young children, but do not be too quick to discount the more involved projects for students in lower grades. With a little ingenuity, these projects can be modified for most age groups. For instance, a project that calls for fabric, needle, and thread can be made appropriate for even very young students simply by using construction paper and glue instead.

A little extra effort in preparation can also help you eliminate the more complex or time-consuming steps of many projects. For example, instead of asking children to measure and cut out cardboard or fabric pieces to certain dimensions in the classroom, you can prepare these materials in advance. As a rule, making a project yourself before presenting it to a class is a good idea. Your finished work will help students understand the instructions and inspire them to charge ahead. It will also give you a sense of how long the project will take with your students and whether you need to adapt the lesson in any way for your class.

It is my hope that teachers will view these projects as a jumping-off point. In my own experience, I've found that the best way to keep any program fresh is to create new lessons myself. You will be amazed at how merely accumulating materials for these projects will trigger your creativity. You will not only start thinking of different ways to use and modify these lessons, but also develop ideas for new projects. (The sources listed in the bibliography can lend you additional inspiration.) With a little practice, you can learn to translate an idea or object you have seen into methods and materials that can be worked in the classroom.

Aside from the fun of coming up with new ideas, there is another important benefit from such creative thinking. Children can sense a teacher's enthusiasm for a project, and the excitement is contagious. If a project sparks your imagination, it is likely to do the same for your students.

– Susan Major-Tingey

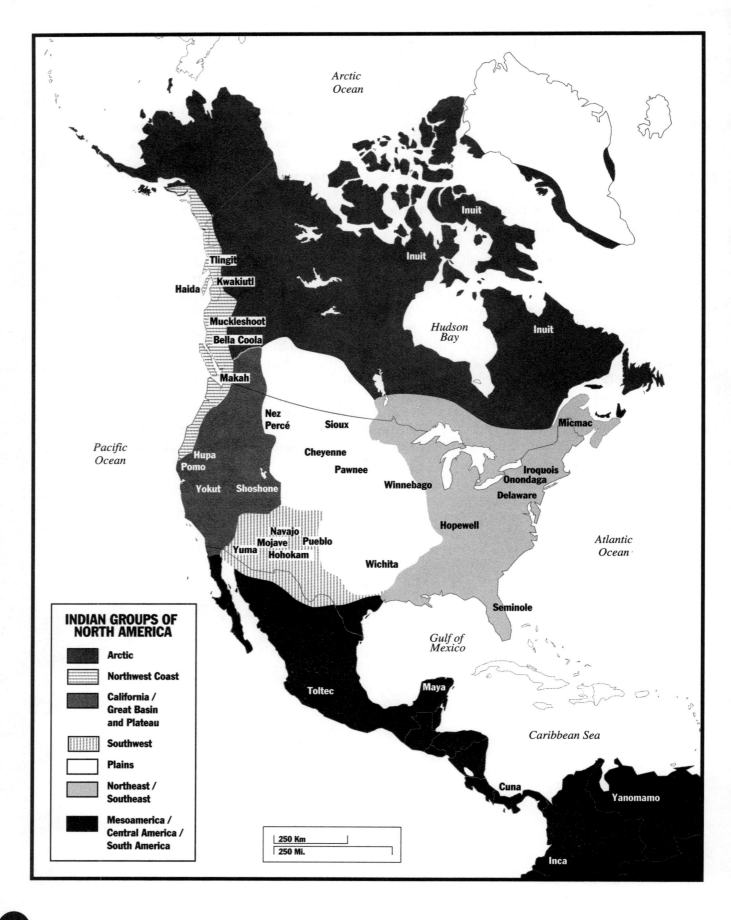

INDIAN GROUPS OF NORTH AMERICA

- Arctic
- Northwest Coast
- California / Great Basin and Plateau
- Southwest
- Plains
- Northeast / Southeast
- Mesoamerica / Central America / South America

250 Km
250 Mi.

Arctic Ocean

Pacific Ocean

Atlantic Ocean

Hudson Bay

Gulf of Mexico

Caribbean Sea

Inuit
Inuit
Inuit

Tlingit
Kwakiutl
Haida
Muckleshoot
Bella Coola
Makah

Nez Percé
Sioux
Cheyenne
Pawnee
Winnebago

Micmac
Iroquois
Onondaga
Delaware

Hupa
Pomo
Yokut
Shoshone

Hopewell

Navajo
Mojave
Pueblo
Yuma
Hohokam
Wichita

Seminole

Toltec
Maya

Cuna
Yanomamo

Inca

Northeast and Southeast

LONGHOUSE

The Delaware Indians of the mid-Atlantic coast lived in longhouses, a type of dwelling also made by the Iroquois and other northeastern tribes. To build a longhouse, these Indians cleared a large rectangular expanse of earth, then placed wooden poles in the ground along the long sides of the rectangle. The poles were bent toward each other to create a series of arcs, onto which branches were lashed horizontally and vertically. Bark shingles were then secured over the frame to keep the wind and rain out. Only the door openings on both ends were left uncovered. The width of longhouses was always about 18 to 25 feet, but their length varied depending on the number of people they housed. Some longhouses were 50 feet long, while others stretched nearly 200 feet.

Longhouse inhabitants usually included several related families, the members of which all belonged to the same clan. (There were three clans among the Delawares, symbolized by the turkey, wolf, and turtle). Each family had its own living space along one side of the interior. In the center of the longhouse was a row of fires–about one every five feet–that were used for cooking and to provide warmth. Families living opposite from one another usually shared a hearth.

MATERIALS

shoe box lid

scissors

thin twigs

glue

masking tape

gray and brown construction paper

DIRECTIONS

1. Cut out a rectangular slits at both ends of the shoe box lid. These slits will represent the longhouse doors.

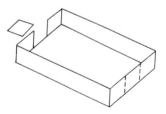

2. Next tape the bottom of the twigs to the four corners of the lid, as shown. To keep the twigs secure, wrap the tape around both the twig and the side of the box.

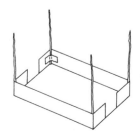

3. Using the same method, tape (three) twigs to the middle of each of the long sides of the cover.

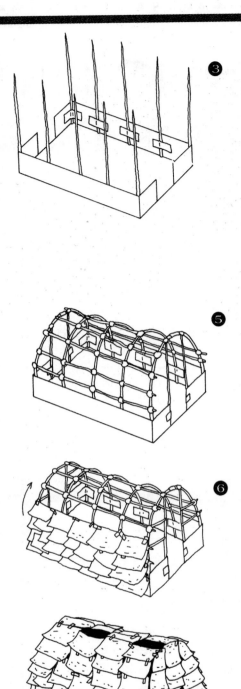

4. Next, bend the twigs on opposite sides of the cover and tape them at the tips as shown below. This will create a frame of five arches.

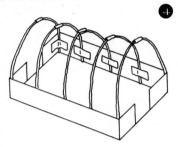

5. Tape twigs horizontally to the sides and top of the frame. On each end, tape twigs vertically to the side of the door openings. Tape additional twigs horizontally to make the walls.

6. Tear construction paper into rectangles about 1" x 2" to create bark shingles. Starting at the bottom, glue them to the box cover and up the sides of the frame. Each new row of shingles should overlap the previous row. Do not cover the door openings. Also, leave a series of small openings along the center of the top to represent smoke holes.

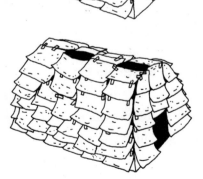

7. Draw on construction paper one of the three clan symbols—the turtle, the wolf, or the turkey—and cut it out. Use the cutout symbol to trace a second one, and cut it out. Glue one symbol over each doorway.

TIP: Before beginning the project, briefly store your glue in the freezer to make it thicker, thus easier to use.

Mica Hand Cutouts

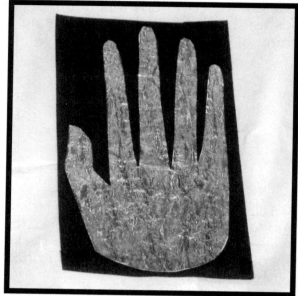

The culture of the prehistoric Hopewell Indians flourished in the Ohio River valley from about 300 B.C. to A.D. 700. The artifacts uncovered by archaeologists show that the Hopewell were extremely skilled craftspeople. They carved pipes from stone, shaped pottery from clay, and decorated jewelry and bowls with bits of shell and stone. But their most unique works were their cutouts. These simple flat shapes (often animals or human faces in profile) were made by carefully chipping a piece of copper or mica with a flint tool. The activity below is inspired by a mica cutout of a hand with long, tapering fingers and a bent thumb.

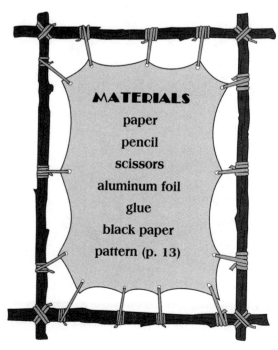

MATERIALS

paper

pencil

scissors

aluminum foil

glue

black paper

pattern (p. 13)

DIRECTIONS

1. Trace around one hand (with your thumb bent) on a sheet of paper. Adjust the sketch by making your palm and fingers longer. (If you're having difficulty drawing, try using the template on the opposite page.)

2. Next, cut out the paper hand and glue it to the foil. A weight (such as a heavy book) can be used to keep the hand flat as it dries.

3. Carefully trim the foil around the hand.

4. Glue the foil hand on to black paper. When it dries, your mica hand is ready to display!

TRY THIS: Miniature foil hands can be glued to colored cardboard and worn as a pendant.

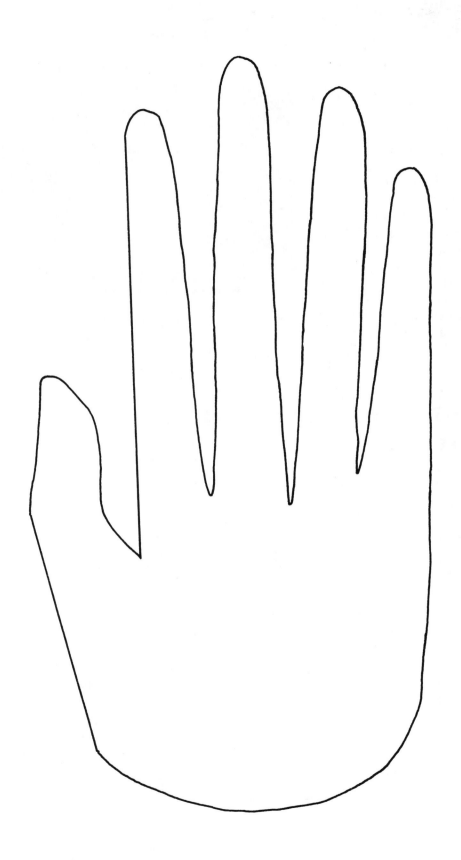

$ILVER WORK

In the seventeenth century, French and Dutch colonists introduced the Iroquois to the art of silversmithing. At first, Iroquois smiths melted down silver dollars and Mexican silver coins for raw material. Later European traders provided them with sheets of ingot silver and German silver—an alloy that contained copper, nickel, and zinc. More durable and less costly than pure silver, German silver was also relatively thin and flat so it could be cut and shaped more easily. One of the Iroquois' favorite uses for German silver was making broad bands decorated with cutouts and engraved designs. They strapped these bands around their gustowehs, traditional hats that they had previously adorned with porcupine quill embroidery.

PROJECT ONE: HEADBAND

DIRECTIONS

1. Cut a piece of cardboard 3" wide and several inches longer than the circumference of your head.

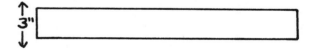

2. Cover the cardboard with glue, and wrap aluminum foil around it. A weight (such as a heavy book) can be used to keep it flat as it dries. To avoid getting any glue on to the book, you might want to first place your strip of foil in between sheets of newspaper.

3. Then fold the strip of paper in half (foil inside) and then in half again. Continue until the folded paper is slightly more than 1" long.

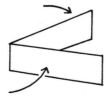

MATERIALS

lightweight cardboard,
scissors, glue

aluminum foil

newspaper

3"-wide strip of paper
(long enough to go
around head)

paper punch, pencil

black marker

4. With a pencil, draw a convex arc on one end of the paper.

5. Cut along the line, and open up the paper. This is called a scalloped edge because it looks like many little scallop shells lined up in a row.

6. Using a paper punch, experiment with punching out overlapping holes to create different shapes.

7. Use markers to create a design on the foil. Permanent black markers work best.

8. Wrap the silver piece around your forehead. Form a headband by gluing down the overlap. Once the glue dries, your headband is ready to wear!

PROJECT TWO: SILVER BROOCH

MATERIALS

3" square of oaktag • silver and black crayons • glue • safety pin

DIRECTIONS

1. Using the silver crayon, draw V shapes and overlapping circles on the oaktag.

2. Color in the background with the black crayon. Press firmly so that the crayoned surface is shiny.

3. Glue the safety pin to the back of the colored square.

WAMPUM BELT

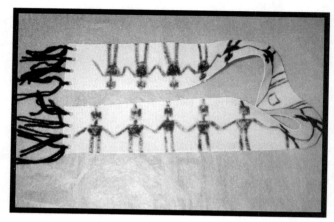

Like most Native American peoples, the Indians of the Iroquois Confederacy had no written language. Instead of recording their history and traditions in books, they passed down this knowledge orally from generation to generation. Although Iroquois historians had to have incredible powers of recall to preserve the many stories of their people, they also relied on wampum belts as memory aids. These belts, woven from strings of purple and white shell beads, were made to commemorate special events. The figures and designs formed by the beads represented certain aspects of what had occurred. By scanning the wampum belt, knowledgeable elders could "read" the patterns and reconstruct the event in startling detail.

The project below is patterned after a famous wampum belt that was made as a record of a peace treaty between the Iroquois Confederacy and the U.S. government following the American Revolution. The longest wampum belt in existence, its 10,000 beads form 13 figures, which symbolize the original 13 states. Two smaller figures representing Iroquois leaders flank a stylized longhouse—the traditional dwelling of the Iroquois.

MATERIALS

sturdy fabric
(such as canvas)
or oaktag

markers

paper punch

yarn

DIRECTIONS

1. Cut a strip of fabric or oaktag to fit around your waist.

2. Using markers, draw figures on the fabric or oaktag. The figures should have wide shoulders and tapered torsos. Single lines can stand for the human legs and arms and the outline of the longhouse.

3. At each end of the belt, punch a line of holes. String yarn through the holes, and tie it to create a yarn fringe. If you plan to wear the belt, make an 18" yarn tie on both ends.

TRY THIS: Students can create their own wampum belt designs to commemorate important school events or personal accomplishments.

FRIENDSHIP NECKLACE

By Iroquois custom, when a person says something important, he or she gives the listener a special gift. For hundreds of years, strings of white and purple shell beads known as wampum have been used for this purpose. A gift of wampum is thought to confirm the truth of a statement and the sincerity of its speaker. The combination of colors on the string often carries an additional message. For instance, a particular pattern may represent the name of the gift giver or the recipient.

DIRECTIONS

1. Design your own pattern for stringing the white and purple beads. For instance, you may alternate one white with two purples, three whites with one purple, etc.

2. Make several strings of beads in your pattern.

3. Exchange strings of beads with several classmates. (Each student should end up with strings of several different patterns of beads, each representing a different classmate.)

4. Tie the strings of beads together, and tape them onto a string or piece of yarn to make a necklace.

5. Color the tape with markers.

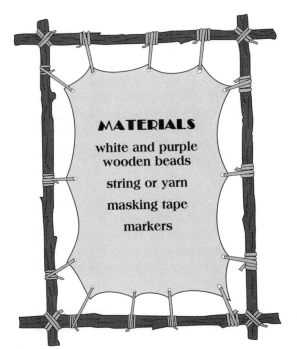

MATERIALS

white and purple wooden beads

string or yarn

masking tape

markers

TIP: (For coloring wooden beads) Use markers if the wooden beads are unlacquered and acrylic paint if they are lacquered.

Tree of the Great Peace

Probably in the late 1500s, the mighty League of the Iroquois was founded. Its members were five tribes living in present-day New York—the Mohawks, Oneidas, Onondagas, Cayugas, and Senecas. (In 1722, they were joined by the Tuscarora Indians.) Before the league was formed, these tribes had long fought among themselves. According to Iroquois legend, they became allies after the great prophet Deganawida had a vision, in which he saw these warring groups united beneath the sheltering branches of the Tree of the Great Peace. On top of this tree was an eagle that screamed out to warn the people of any approaching danger.

The Tree of the Great Peace remains a powerful symbol for the Iroquois. In 1992, an Onondaga artist depicted it in a luminous stone sculpture colored pale green at the base and a butterscotch shade at the top. In this work, the tree is supported by a turtle, an emblem of a clan found among all of the Iroquois tribes. The turtle also represents longevity and eternal life.

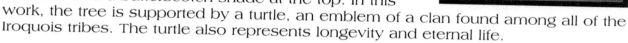

PROJECT ONE: WATERCOLOR

MATERIALS

white paper

pencil

watercolors

DIRECTIONS

1. On a sheet of white paper, draw the turtle, tree, and eagle (or use the template on p. 20).

2. Mix a butterscotch color on the cover of your paint box. Start with some yellow paint, and add small amounts of orange until the color is the same as a piece of butterscotch candy. (You may want to have butterscotch candy on hand for comparison.)

3. Mix a light green color on the cover of your paint box by combining about a teaspoon of water and a dab of green paint. (If the color is too strong, you can make it duller by adding a touch of orange, green's complementary color.)

4. Paint the drawing, starting with the butterscotch color at the top and the light green at the bottom. Where the colors meet, blend them together with the brush to form a new color. (Do not worry if the color spreads beyond the lines of the drawing.) Allow the paint to dry.

5. Cut out the drawing, and tape it to a window. When the light shines through the paper, the drawing will seem to glow!

PROJECT TWO: MELTED CRAYON DRAWING

MATERIALS

white paper • pencil • crayons • newspaper • iron

DIRECTIONS

1. On a sheet of white paper sketch (or use the pattern on p. 20) the turtle, tree, and eagle lightly in pencil.

2. Using crayons, color the turtle light green and the eagle yellow-orange. Color the top of the tree yellow-orange; the bottom, light green; and the middle, a blend of the two colors. (Press down hard with the crayons to build up a thick layer of wax.)

3. Place the drawings between newspaper, and run an electric iron over the top. (For safety's sake, an adult should do the ironing for young children.) The heat from the iron will melt the crayon wax, making the paper translucent.

4. Tape the drawing to a window. The drawing will seem to glow as light comes through the paper!

CONICAL WIGWAM

Wigwams were one of the most common types of dwelling among the Indians of the Northeast and the Great Lakes region. All the materials needed to build a wigwam were easily collected from the great forests that covered these areas. The dwelling's frame was generally made from saplings; its walls were constructed from overlapping sheets of birch, elm, or chestnut bark or mats woven from reeds or grass. In the winter, wigwam builders sometimes added a layer of grass between the frame and the covering. With this insulation in place and a fire burning in its center, a wigwam stayed warm and dry even during the most bitter snowstorm.

Most wigwams were dome shaped. However, some tribes living along the northern Atlantic coast, such as the Micmacs of Nova Scotia, built conical wigwams. The shape of these dwellings resembles that of the tipi, the favored housing type of the Indians of the Great Plains.

PROJECT ONE: FREE-STANDING

MATERIALS

cardboard

compass, pencil

scissors, tape

12 thin twigs

rubber band

brown paper bags

white & brown paper

black markers

DIRECTIONS

1. Draw an 8" circle on the piece of cardboard.

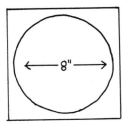

2. Using the sharp point of the scissors, make 12 evenly spaced holes alongside the edge of the circle. (Important: An adult should make the holes for young children.)

3. Place the thicker ends of twigs in the holes, pushing them through the lid until they touch the bottom of the box.

4. Tie the tops of twigs together with a rubberband.

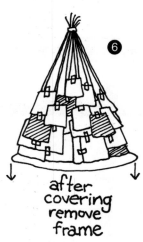

5. Wrap the frame using large pieces of the brown paper bag.

cover bottom

6. Tear up white and brown paper into 1-inch squares. Tape pieces (overlapping them somewhat) onto the frame covered with the paper bag pieces.

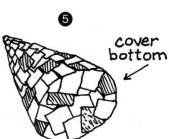

after covering remove frame

7. Use black markers to add birch-bark lines to the white and construction paper.

8. Cut out an opening for the door. Save the cutout piece, and tape it to a slightly larger paper. (Tape this piece over the top of the opening to create the entry flap.)

doorway

QUILLWORK BOX

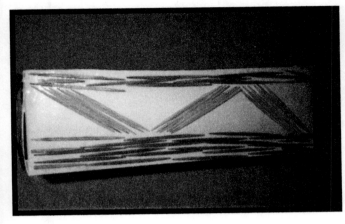

Porcupine quillwork is a decorative technique unique to the Indians of North America. It was practiced by many tribes in the Northeast, the natural habitat of the porcupine. However, through trade, Indians far to the south and east obtained quills and developed their own forms of this craft.

Quillwork required a great deal of time, patience, and skill. Once the quills were collected (an easy task because the average porcupine has more than 30,000), they had to be sorted by size, softened in water, colored with vegetable and mineral dyes, and flattened. In the method of quillwork favored by Plains Indians, the prepared quills—each about 5" long—were twisted around sinew or thread to create one long strand. The strand was then used to embroider tiny stitches into a piece of hide or cloth to make an appliqué that could be sewn onto a garment or bag. Another technique involved threading individual quills through objects made of birch bark. Masters of this method, the Micmac Indians made small boxes covered with colorful geometric designs.

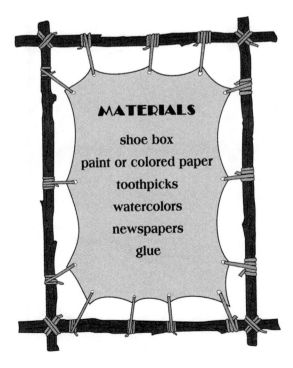

MATERIALS

shoe box

paint or colored paper

toothpicks

watercolors

newspapers

glue

DIRECTIONS

1. Paint the box or cover it with paper so that it is a solid color. If using paints, allow the paint to dry.

2. Paint toothpicks with watercolors, and place them on newspaper to dry.

3. Turn the box on its side.

4. Glue several rows of toothpicks parallel to the top of the box.

5. Glue other toothpicks in a zigzag pattern next to the parallel toothpicks.

6. Glue several rows of toothpicks parallel to the bottom of the box.

CANOE

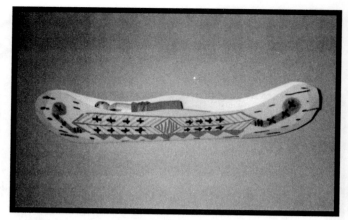

The Micmac Indians spent the spring and summer fishing in the rivers that flowed through their lands along the coast of eastern Canada. They navigated these waterways in long, narrow canoes made from the bark of the birch tree. Birchbark canoes were light to carry but sturdy enough to paddle through rough waters. In fact, they were so strong that the Micmacs sometimes rode them into the Atlantic Ocean while hunting for seals. To keep their canoes from flooding when battered with waves, the Micmacs designed them with tightly closed ends and a slight hump in the middle of each side.

DIRECTIONS

1. Fold a piece of oaktag in half.

2. On the oaktag, draw the shape of a canoe with the bottom of the boat on the fold. The ends of the canoe should be rounded, and the

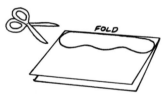

FOLD

hump in the middle about the same height as the top of the two ends. If you don't want to draw your own, use the template on the opposite page.

3. Cut out the canoe, leaving the fold intact.

4. Draw black lines of various lengths, all in the same direction, to simulate the look of birch bark.

5. Tape together the curves at the front and back of the canoe's bottom. Add tape along the curve on the inside of the canoe to help it keep its shape.

6. With markers, draw a face and other details on a clothespin figure. Place your figurine inside the canoe.

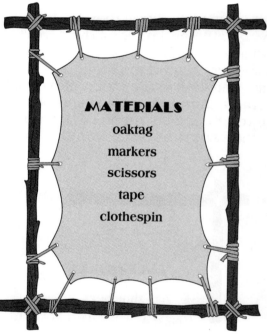

MATERIALS

oaktag

markers

scissors

tape

clothespin

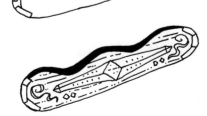

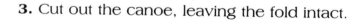

TRY THIS: Your miniature canoe can be used as a desktop pen-and-pencil holder!

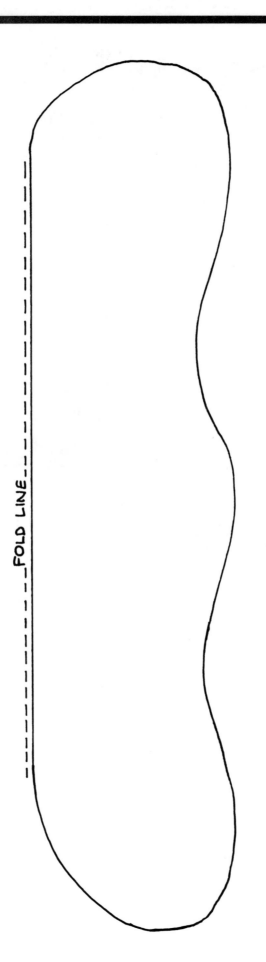

FOLD LINE

WOMAN'S CAPE

Living in the forests along the shores of Lake Superior and Lake Huron, the Ojibwas needed warm clothing in order to stay comfortable during the region's frigid winters. The men of the tribe hunted animals to obtain the skins and furs from which they made these clothes. The women were responsible for tanning the skins and sewing them into shirts, pants, dresses, and capes, which they wore over their heads when the weather was particularly harsh. Women also had the job of decorating special pieces of clothing, often by forming ornate floral designs from colored beads or fabric appliques. The project below is modeled after an Ojibwa woman's cape sewn in the 1850s and adorned with fringe and a pattern of leaves made out of tiny seed beads.

MATERIALS

tape measure

brown wrapping paper

scissors, pins

fabric

markers

green felt or construction paper

DIRECTIONS

1. Measure the length of a student's back from shoulder to shoulder. (Probably only one measurement needs to be taken, because it will be similar for all the students in the class.) Add 6" to the measurement, and (cut a circle with this diameter out of brown wrapping paper.)

2. Cut a circle with a 7" diameter out of the center of the paper pattern.

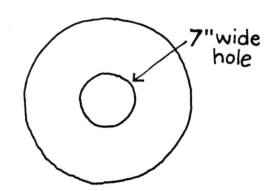

7"wide hole

3. Pin the paper circle to the fabric, and cut the fabric around the pattern.

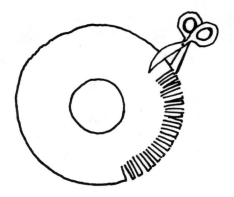

4. Cut a series of 3" slits around the edge of the fabric to make fringe.

5. Decorate your cape using markers. You might want to glue on decorative pieces too.

6. When you're finished decorating your cape, cut a 6" slit down the front of the fabric piece.

7. Your cape is ready to wear!

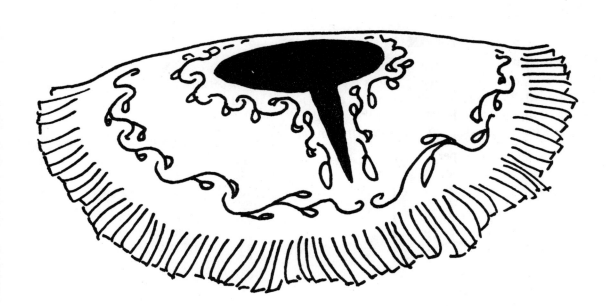

CHICKEE

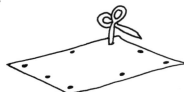

The Seminoles developed a shelter that was ideal for their hot and swampy homeland in southeastern Florida. Known as a chickee, this rectangular dwelling was built from a frame of wooden poles that was left open at the sides. Only the roof was thatched, usually with palmetto *fronds* (leaves), although straw or rushes were used if they were plentiful. The floor of the chickee was a platform of split palmetto logs elevated 30 inches above the ground.

Because of their design, chickees were surprisingly cool and comfortable. The thatched roof shielded the interior from the region's torrential rains and harsh sun, while the open sides and raised platform allowed breezes to circulate through and under the house. The height of the floor also protected the inhabitants from other hazards of their environment—from flood tides to unwelcome visits from swamp snakes and alligators.

DIRECTIONS

1. Punch holes in the four corners and midway on the sides of both pieces of poster board. Be sure that the holes are at least 1/4" in from all edges.

2. Fit twigs into the four corner holes of the smaller piece of poster board, which will be the chickee's floor. Push each twig through so that about 1" worth of twig extends through each hole. Secure the cardboard in place with masking tape. Part of each piece of tape should be on the twig and part on the underside of the poster board.

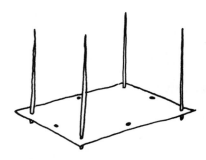

3. Add a twig crossbeam on both ends of the structure, joining it at the corners with thin pieces of masking tape wrapped around both twigs. This creates a sturdy rectangle of twigs on both ends of the structure.

MATERIALS

poster board
(6" x 9" and
8" x 9" pieces)

paper punch

twigs

masking tape

garden clippers

glue

grass

4. Fit twigs into the holes punched midway on all four sides. The twigs in the sides will need to be taller than the ones on the ends. Secure twigs to poster board with thin pieces of tape.

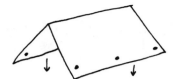

5. Fold the 8" x 9" piece of poster board in half to form the roof. Slip the ends of the vertical poles into the holes in the roof, and secure them with tape on the underside.

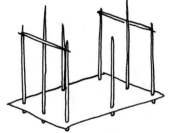

6. Snip off the twig ends with garden clippers. Cover the ends and the area around them with tape to add stability.

7. Cover the roof with glue, and apply grass. Dry. Add a second application of glue and grass to cover places missed the first time.

TIPS:

1) Although most of the model can be assembled without assistance, students might find it helpful to work with a partner. Partners can take turns, one holding the model in place while the other glues or connects the pieces together.

2) Using twigs will create the most authentic model. However, wooden dowels, chopsticks, or pencils can be used instead. If using pencils, you may choose to paint them a natural wood color or to scrape or sand off the yellow paint covering them.

BANDOLIER BAG

Popular with many eastern tribes, bandolier bags were probably adapted from packs worn by English military officers. More decorative than functional, these large, flat, rectangular bags with wide shoulder straps were worn by men during special occasions. Some men put on as many as seven bags at once, but more often, they wore only one or occasionally two, with the straps crossing on the chest and the back.

Bandolier bags were decorated with geometric or floral patterns, usually made from beads, dyed porcupine quills, or embroidered fabric appliqués. The beaded Seminole bag on which this project is based was made in the early 1800s. Two different designs appeared on the strap, and the bag's bottom edge was adorned with tassels or fringe.

DIRECTIONS

1. Fold up the bottom third of the red felt, and stitch (or staple) it to the middle third at the sides.

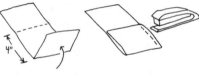

2. Cut off the corners of the top third, and fold it down over the bag to create a triangular flap.

3. Cut out blue and white felt shapes, and glue them to the flap and bottom corners of the bag. Allow the glue to dry.

4. Add yarn tassels and, if desired, a braided yarn strap.

MATERIALS

red felt (9" x 12" piece)

blue and white felt
(3" x 9" pieces)

needle and thread
or stapler

glue, yarn

TIP: This project can be made using paper instead of felt.

CALENDAR STICK

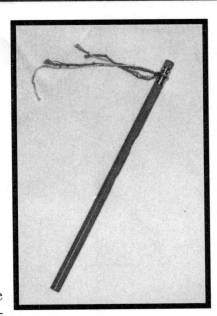

The Winnebago Indians used calendar sticks to record the passing of time before important events—from births and deaths to ceremonies to natural wonders, such as meteor showers and eclipses. Days, months, and years were usually represented with notches cut into these sticks. Strands of beads or strings tied with knots were attached to them to symbolize special features of these occasions. Some calendar sticks were passed on from generation to generation, thereby becoming visual reminders of the history of the tribe.

DIRECTIONS

1. String beads or knot thread, and tie them to the top of a pencil or a stick.

2. Color in the notches to count off the days before a school event or vacation.

TRY THIS: While making this project, have a classroom discussion about various methods people have used to record the passing of time, including clocks, time lines, growth charts, hourglasses, and sundials.

MATERIALS
pencil
beads
thread
markers

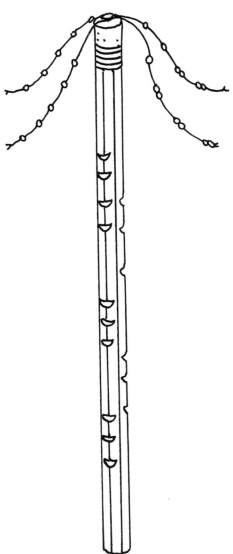

GREAT PLAINS

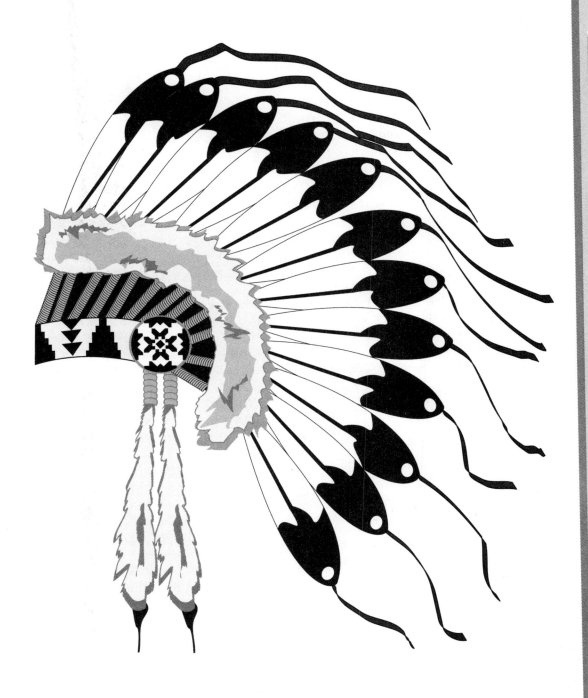

TIPI

Like most Indian groups of the Great Plains—including the Sioux, Apaches, Kiowas, and the Blackfeet—the Cheyenne Indians lived in cone-shaped houses known as tipis. Tipis were comfortable dwellings in any weather, no matter how harsh. In the winter, they kept out the freezing wind and snow, while holding in the heat of a fire. In the summer, they stayed cool even in the blazing sun. But even more important to these Indians was the tipi's portability. During the hunting season, they had to move constantly as they followed the buffalo herds that roamed through the Plains. For such a mobile people, the tipi was an ideal dwelling. A tipi could be disassembled quickly and harnessed to the back of a horse for easy transport. Once a new hunting camp was reached, the tipi could be erected in less than an hour.

A tipi was made from a frame of wooden poles that were embedded in the ground at the bottom and tied together near the top, forming a cone. The frame was then covered by 10 to 20 buffalo hides that had been sewn into a semicircle. Women were responsible for cleaning and tanning the hides and sewing the covers. The job of decorating the covers, however, fell to men. Sometimes they painted tipis with pictures of their battle exploits or another feat of which they were especially proud. At other times, they used abstract designs that they had seen in a dream or a vision. An artist often reserved particularly distinctive designs for the top of his tipi, so that when he returned from a hunting expedition, he could easily identify his home from a distance.

MATERIALS

yellowish parchment paper

tape, glue, scissors

10 toothpicks

twig

fabric

markers

DIRECTIONS

1. Roll a sheet of parchment paper to form a cone, and tape it in front temporarily.

GLUE

2. Using a small amount of glue on your fingertip, glue down the edge of the paper on the inside of the cone, so that it keeps its form and does not unroll.

3. Near the top, pinch the cone (on side where the flap is located). Snip the top to create a smoke hole.

4. Trim the bottom of the cone so that it stands fairly straight. Cut as little as possible to ensure that the tipi is large enough to decorate easily.

5. Place toothpicks on a 2" piece of tape. Roll up the tape, and pinch it so that the toothpicks are joined at the bottom, yet separate at the top.

6. Place cone on its side, and insert the top of the toothpicks through the smoke hole. Glue the tape joining the toothpicks to the top on the cone.

7. Glue the stick to the side flap. The stick may be held in place temporarily with tape. Allow the glue to dry completely. (You may prefer to trim the paper and instead add a fabric flap, which will be easier to manipulate.)

8. Decorate the tipi with markers. Cheyenne tipi designs incorporated crosses, triangles, zigzags, forks, V's, circles, bands of different colors, and lines of dots.

9. Open the side flap, and, if necessary, trim the cone to create a triangular-shaped entrance.

10. Tape or glue a small piece of fabric inside the opening to create a dew cloth—a lining that insulated the inside of a tipi from dew and rain. (Twist the stick to the back to close the flap over the smoke hole.)

TIP: This tipi may be made with oaktag, which produces a more sturdy, although less translucent, model. If using oaktag, glue down both the inside and outside flaps. Because oaktag is stiff and inflexible, use a piece of fabric to create the entrance flap.

BAG AND POUCH

The Cheyennes spent most of the year traveling from hunting camp to hunting camp. They carried few possessions, but those they did were carefully stored in sturdy leather bags, which they painted with colorful geometric designs. Smaller bags and pouches made to hold particularly treasured objects often were adorned with colorful glass beads, yarn, and metal trinkets that the Cheyenne obtained from non-Indian traders. For example, men crafted special pouches to carry their face paints, which they applied to their cheeks and foreheads before going into battle and performing certain ceremonies.

PROJECT ONE: DECORATED BAG

DIRECTIONS

1. Cut two rectangles of the same size from felt of one color.

2. Cut six vertical slits about an inch from one end of one of the pieces of felt.

3. Thread the rawhide through the slits.

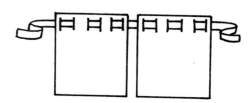

4. Pin the two pieces of felt together, and sew around the sides and the bottom to create a bag.

MATERIALS

felt in several colors

scissors

rawhide shoelace
or belt

pins

needle and thread

pencil, paper

glue

newspaper

5. Make paper patterns of geometric shapes—triangles, rectangles, crosses, etc.—and pin them to other colors of felt. Cut out the felt shapes.

6. Spread glue sparingly around the edges of the felt shapes, and glue them to the bag.

7. Put the bag between sheets of newspaper, and place a weight on top. Allow the glue to dry.

PROJECT TWO: MAN'S POUCH

MATERIALS

oaktag • pencil • scissors • long rawhide shoelace • stapler • paper punch • yarn newspaper

DIRECTIONS

1. Draw and cut two large U-shapes (of equal size) on oaktag. These pieces are the front and back of your pouch.

2. Draw a 1/4" border around the curved part of each shape.

3. Tie the ends of the rawhide together to make a carrying strap. Staple the strap to one of the oaktag U shapes.

4. Staple the two oaktag pieces together along the border, leaving the top open. Leave about 1/2" between the staples.

5. Punch holes in between the staples.

6. Cut the yarn in 3" pieces. Run the pieces through the holes and tie them to create fringe.

EARTH LODGE

Except for during their winter hunting expeditions, the Pawnee Indians inhabited large villages in what is now Kansas and Nebraska. Like other Indian groups who settled along the rivers of the central and northern Plains, such as the Mandans and the Hidatsas, the Pawnees lived in earth lodges. These houses, which looked like great domes of dirt, were constructed from a frame of wooden poles covered with sod. Inside the entrance of each lodge was a short, narrow passageway that led to a large circular room. The entrance always faced the east, so that

the morning light would fill the room and remind the dwellers of the god of light and fire. In addition to permitting hearth fire smoke to escape the dwelling, a hole at the top of the dome allowed the Pawnees to look up and see the sky, which linked them to the god of the heavens.

In the spring and fall, the Pawnees built special ceremonial lodges. During rituals held there, dancers acted out the tribe's myths about supernatural beings whom the Pawnees believed lived on earth. These beings took the form of animals and were thought to live in their own earth lodges far beyond the Pawnees' villages.

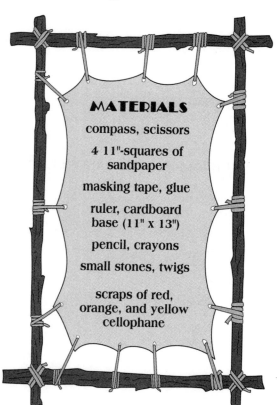

MATERIALS

compass, scissors

4 11"-squares of sandpaper

masking tape, glue

ruler, cardboard base (11" x 13")

pencil, crayons

small stones, twigs

scraps of red, orange, and yellow cellophane

PROJECT ONE: EARTH LODGE WITH ROOF AND FIRE

DIRECTIONS

1. On the back of one of the pieces of sandpaper draw a circle with an 11" diameter. Cut it out.

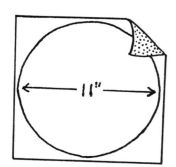

2. Draw a circle with a 2" diameter in the center of the larger circle. Make a straight cut from the side to the edge of the inner circle. Cut out the inner circle, and remove it.

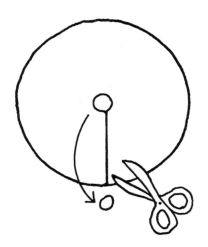

3. Roll the circle into a squat cone, with the rough surface of the sandpaper on the outside. Overlap the cut edges, and tape them in place on inside of the cone. This will be the dwelling's roof.

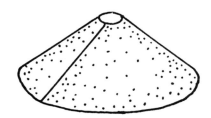

4. Cut a square of sandpaper in half to create two 5 1/2" x 11" rectangles. Roll one up to form a large, short cylinder, again keeping the rough surface of the paper on the outside. (The diameter of the cylinder should be smaller than that of the cone.) Tape the edges in place on the inside of the cylinder. This will form the sides of the structure.

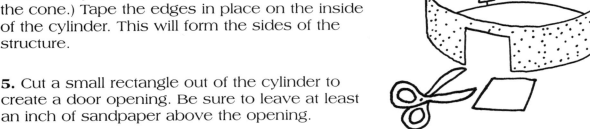

5. Cut a small rectangle out of the cylinder to create a door opening. Be sure to leave at least an inch of sandpaper above the opening.

6. Fold a 3"-wide piece of sandpaper to create an arch that fits your doorway. See diagram. Remember: The rough surface goes on the outside.

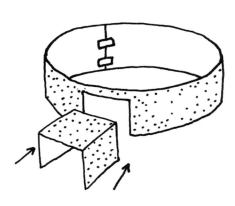
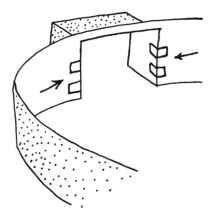

7. Tape it to the cylinder so that it surrounds the door opening.

8. Apply the roof to the cylinder and place it on a cardboard base. Your Pawnee earth lodge is finished!

9. To make your lodge look more authentic, paint the cardboard base the same color as the lodge. When it dries, add sand, stones and twigs.

10. To make a fire inside earth lodge, cut pieces of cellophane to create spiky edges that resemble flames. Glue the cellophane to some twigs. Place your fire inside, at the center of the lodge.

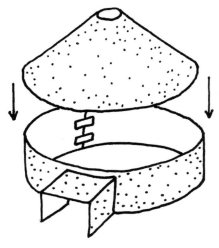

TIP: If possible, do this project in two sessions. On the first day, allow about an hour to make the oaktag and tape structure. On the second day, set up a gluing station in the room, and allow one student at a time to add the sand coating to their lodges while the others do desk work.

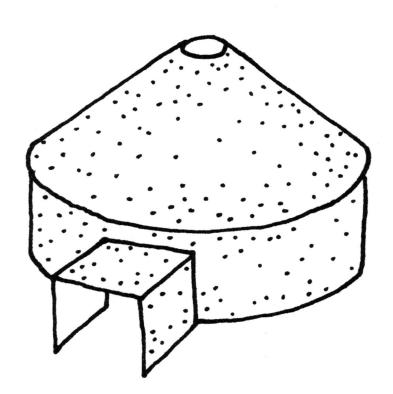

DANCER'S ANKLET

For most Indian people, including the Sioux, dancing is more than a form of entertainment. It is a crucial part of the religious ceremonies that they have performed for hundreds of years. Traditionally, ceremonial dancing helped the Sioux prepare for the hunt, brace themselves for battle, and celebrate the natural world.

Sioux dancers often wore colorful costumes adorned with baubles they made themselves from bones or shells or with metal bells they obtained from non-Indians. Dangling from the dancers' arms and legs, these decorations not only enhanced the dancers' movements, but also provided musical accompaniment as they jangled and rattled together.

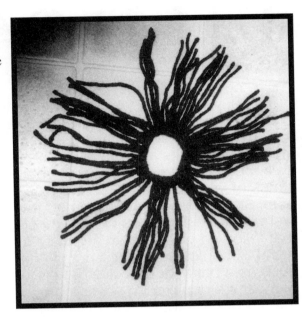

DIRECTIONS

1. Wrap yarn around the 4-inch cardboard square repeatedly. Cut the yarn along one edge to produce 8" lengths of yarn.

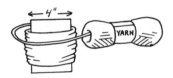 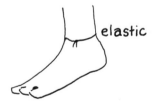

2. Cut a piece of elastic long enough to wrap comfortably around your ankle. Tie the two ends together. Remove from your ankle.

3. Fold a piece of yarn in half. Place the loop at the middle under the elastic, and bring the ends through the loop as shown.

4. Repeat until the elastic is covered with fringe.

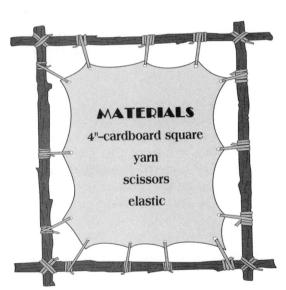

MATERIALS

4"-cardboard square

yarn

scissors

elastic

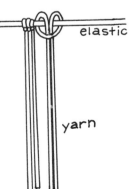

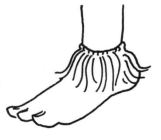

PICTURE CALENDAR

The Sioux did not have a written language with which they could record important events. Instead they used picture calendars to tell the story of their lives and the history of their tribes. Picture calendars were a series of images painted on a buffalo hide. Sioux artists usually painted the first picture in the hide's center; those that followed were drawn around it in a spiral. A particularly significant event, such as a battle or an eclipse, was sometimes depicted in several pictures. But more often each year was recorded with a single painting.

Only men painted picture calendars. Because they were usually made in the winter—the only season when men were not on the hunt—picture calendars were also known as "winter counts."

MATERIALS

pencil

large manila paper

scissors

tea

brush

markers

yarn

DIRECTIONS

1. Sketch the shape of a buffalo hide on a piece of manila paper, making the sketch as large as possible. (Be sure to include four legs and a tail.) If you don't wish to draw one of your own, use the template on the opposite page.

2. Carefully tear or cut out the shape.

3. Starting in the middle, make a series of drawings, each representing a different event.

4. Paint the paper with strong tea to give it the appearance of an aged, tanned skin. Allow it to dry.

5. Go over the sketches with colored markers.

6. Tie on lengths of yarn to make a fur tuft at the end of the tail.

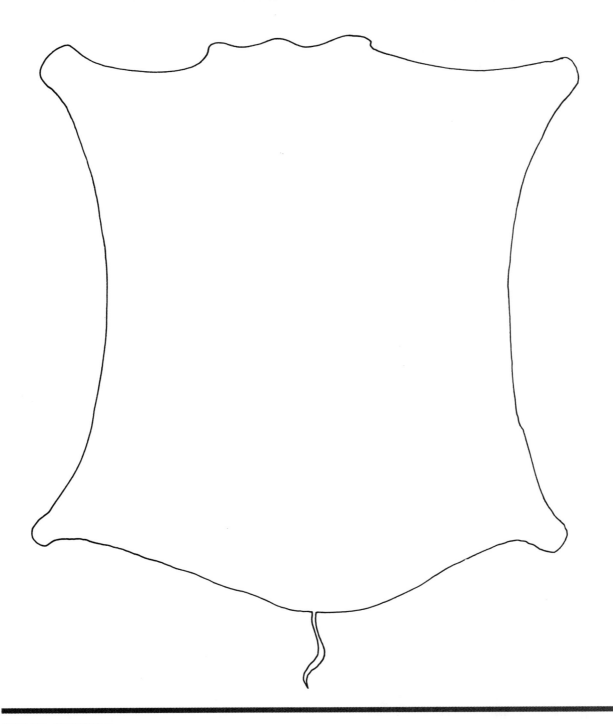

TRY THIS:

1) At the beginning of the school year, ask students to make picture calendars that tell their life story or that illustrate how they spent their summer. These drawings can help classmates get to know one another.

2) Students can also use picture calendars to record the events of the school year, such as field trips, assemblies, etc. At the end of the year, display the pictures at a local library to let the community know what has been going on in your school. Similarly, teachers may keep a picture calendar of happenings in their classroom and reproduce it for students at the school year's end.

Talking Stick

When Sioux leaders were faced with making an important decision that would affect their people, they discussed the matter fully, allowing everyone to have a chance to air an opinion. During such discussions, the leaders passed a special object from one to another. Whoever was holding the object was the designated speaker, and no one was to interrupt him until he had spoken his mind.

Anything could be used to designate a speaker, but often a talking stick was specifically made for this purpose. Some sticks were simply a piece of wood with several feathers attached to one end. More elaborate talking sticks were carefully carved and decorated with ribbons, beads, and wooden animal figures.

DIRECTIONS

Tape feathers to a large stick. To create a fancier talking stick, wind rawhide, ribbons, or yarn around the pencil or stick, and tie on feathers and beads.

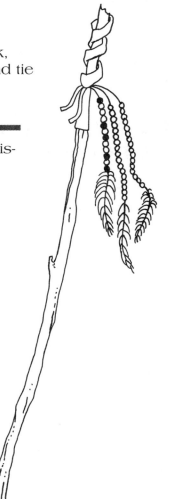

TIP: Keep a talking stick in the classroom for use during discussions. Seat the students in circle, so they can pass the stick quickly and easily from speaker to speaker.

MATERIALS

large stick

feathers

tape

rawhide, ribbon, yarn, beads (optional)

APPLIQUE DESIGNS

Many Indian groups throughout the Northeast, Midwest, and the Great Plains have long adorned their clothing using appliqués—decorated panels that are sewn onto a garment. The earliest appliqués were made from animal skin decorated with dyed porcupine quills. After non-Indians introduced Indians to manufactured goods, Indian artisans began instead using panels of fabric, which they covered with multicolored glass beads or shapes cut from cloth or ribbons. The types of designs they made also changed through contact with non-Indians. Although many craftspeople continued to favor the geometric patterns of their ancestors, others started experimenting with floral designs, which they copied from the patterns on the fabric of non-Indian clothing.

To help them make complicated symmetrical appliqué designs, Dakota Sioux women start by making a paper pattern. They first fold a piece of paper and then cut out different shapes. Many cut their patterns freehand without a specific plan in mind; only when they unfold the paper do they see the design they have created.

PROJECT ONE: PAPER APPLIQUE DESIGN

DIRECTIONS

1. With the colored side on the inside, fold a sheet of origami paper in half. Fold it in half a second time, then fold it diagonally.

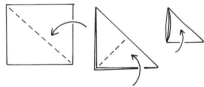

2. Along the thick fold, sketch a design of triangles, diamonds, and curved shapes. If you're having difficulty coming up with a pattern, use the one on page 47.

3. Cut out the shapes, open the sheet, and glue it to a sheet of paper of a contrasting color.

4. If you want to preserve the design, cover it with clear contact paper. A small design also can be glued to a campaign button and covered with clear contact paper. The button then can be worn as a pin.

MATERIALS

Origami paper or thin squares of paper

glue

scissors

pencil

clear contact paper (optional)

campaign button (optional)

TIP: When your students first begin, have them work with a full square of origami paper and concentrate on cutting out geometric shapes. As they become more experienced, encourage them to use smaller sheets of paper and experiment with more complex designs with curved lines.

PROJECT TWO: FELT APPLIQUE DESIGN

MATERIALS

felt in two colors • glue • scissors • paper • T-shirt (optional)

DIRECTIONS

1. Create several paper designs using the method described on the preceding page. Choose your favorite design, and glue it on to a piece of felt. Apply the glue to the paper rather than the felt, using your finger to spread glue thinly over the entire design. If glue is too thick, it will cause the felt to darken and harden.

2. Put each design between newspaper, and stack all the designs on top of one another. Place a heavy book on top of the stack, and allow the designs to dry.

3. Remove the design from the newspaper. Fold the felt slightly where there are holes in the paper, and snip the felt, cutting out all the felt sections without a paper backing.

4. Glue the felt design, paper-backing side down, to a piece of felt of a contrasting color. The felt design also can be glued on to a T-shirt. However, before gluing, be sure to place a protective layer of newspaper inside the shirt, so the glue does not seep through the fabric and onto the back of the shirt.

center

BELT

Lakota men traditionally adorned their long, dark hair with strips of leather decorated with pieces of conch shells. In the nineteenth century, they replaced the shells with silver discs (called conchas), which they obtained through trade. As a man's wealth increased, so did the length of the leather strips and number of silver pieces he wore. When the strips became so long they dragged on the ground, men took to wrapping them around their waists. This practice eventually evolved into a new custom of wearing silver concha belts, which was adopted by both men and women. Today, these belts are still popular with the Lakotas. Women wear long belts so that one end hangs two to three feet below the waist on the left side.

DIRECTIONS

1. Make a belt, with a waist piece and a hanging piece, from the oaktag strips.

2. Lay the belt flat. Color it with a dark crayon.

3. Cover the plastic or cardboard disks with foil, and glue them to the belt. Allow the glue to dry.

MATERIALS

oaktag strips (2" wide)

black crayons

round plastic container covers or cardboard disks

aluminum foil

glue

paper punch

yarn

4. Punch a hole in each side of the back of the waist piece. Attach pieces of yarn through the holes for ties.

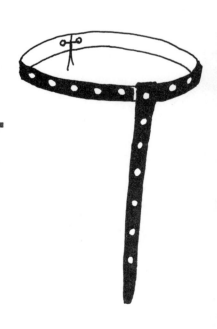

TIP: To make a man's belt, eliminate the hanging piece.

GRASS HOUSE

The Wichita Indians of present-day Oklahoma traditionally lived in villages that contained as many as 70 grass houses. These dwellings had a domed wooden frame made of thick posts and narrow timbers that rose to a point in the dome's center. The Wichitas covered this frame with a thick thatch of grass. Lashed to the front of the door opening was a mat of grass, which could be moved aside easily. In the words of one observer, a finished grass house looked like a "shaggy, large beehive."

According to one of the Wichitas' myths, a messenger of the great spirit Kinnikasus taught the tribe's men and women how to work together to build a grass house. Women were responsible for clearing the round, flat surface of earth on which the house would stand. The men traveled to the forest and gathered the wood from which they constructed a frame. Finally, women collected grass, tied it in bundles, and lashed them to the house. As the Wichitas built a grass house, they prayed to Kinnikasus, asking the spirit to help them perform their work well. They believed that if their houses were strong, their tribe would prosper.

DIRECTIONS

1. Cut the oaktag into 2" strips, and fold them lengthwise. (Overlap strips about 3", and staple them together three times for stability to form a piece that is about 40" long.)

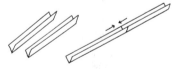

2. Roll the thick oaktag strip into a spiral to make it hold a round shape, and then staple it into a circle. This will give you a sturdy circle base with about a 10" diameter.

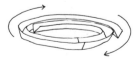

3. Tape twigs to the inside of the oaktag circle. For reinforcement, tape them a second time, placing the tape higher on the twig and bringing the ends over the oaktag at the top.

MATERIALS

oaktag, scissors, stapler, masking tape

freshly cut twigs (about 12" long and less than 1/4" thick)

a round plastic ice cream container or bucket

glue

a large amount of grass

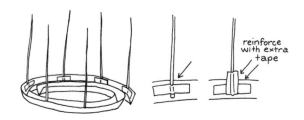

reinforce with extra tape

4. (Twist twigs into a dome shape.) Put the structure into a round container overnight. This step will ensure that the twigs retain their bent shape.

5. Cut l/4"–l/2" oaktag strips, and tape them together to form lengths of about 20". Weave the strips in and out of the poles. When a strip has been woven around the structure completely, overlap the ends and tape them in place. Continue weaving strips until you almost reach the top. Leave space for a smoke hole.

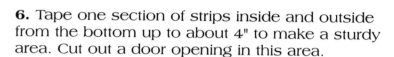

6. Tape one section of strips inside and outside from the bottom up to about 4" to make a sturdy area. Cut out a door opening in this area.

7. Keep the piece of taped oaktag that you cut out, glue grass to it, and allow it to dry. Using thin masking tape, attach this piece to the side of the opening. This will be the door.

8. Gather grass into a large number of 3" long clumps, and tape each together at one end. Tape the clumps to the outside of the frame. Start at the bottom and work around, adding more rows of grass clumps as you move up. Each row should overlap the tape of the previous row. Be sure to leave the smoke hole uncovered.

TIPS:

1) Because of the complexity of this project, give students ample time so that they can do their best work. Consider assigning several students to work together on one model.

2) If you're having a hard time finding dry grass in your area, use oaktag as a substitue. We did. (See picture on page 49.

SOUTHWEST

MOSAICS

The Hohokams were a prehistoric Indian group who lived in what is now southwestern Arizona and northwestern Mexico from about 200 B.C. to A.D. 900. A farming people, the Hohokams settled in villages, the largest of which—now known as Snaketown—was located near the present-day city of Phoenix. During the height of the Hohokam culture, Snaketown covered nearly 300 acres and included more than 100 dwellings.

Much of what we know about the Hohokams was learned from the objects they made. These artifacts, well-preserved in the dry soil of the Southwest, reveal that the Hohokams were accomplished artists. Among their most beautiful works were mosaic bowls made from dried gourds. After cutting a gourd in half, they coated the inside with beeswax. Keeping the wax soft by working in the hot sun, they then embedded tiny objects—bits of shell, turquoise stones, or even kernels of corn or dried peas—to make geometric designs. As the wax cooled, it hardened, holding the inlaid objects firmly in place.

MATERIALS

plastic lid

paper punch

yarn

variety of small decorative objects, such as dried beans, split peas, dried corn kernels, coins

mini-mirrors or silver sequins

liquid glue

PROJECT ONE: WALL OR WINDOW HANGING

DIRECTIONS

1. Punch two holes near the rim of the plastic lid. Tie on a piece of yarn for a hanger.

2. Place the cover on a flat surface. Starting in the center, glue on decorative objects to create a symmetrical design. Keep adding shapes until the area is full. (Tip: Place the glue on the objects rather than on the lid.)

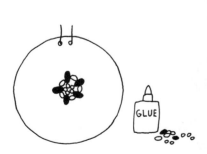

3. Use liquid glue to fill in between the objects for added strength. (Do not apply the glue too thickly, or it will appear cloudy rather than clear when it dries.)

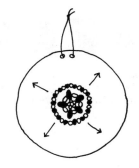

TIPS:

1) Be inventive when collecting decorative objects for this project. A wide variety of objects can be used, but be sure to provide a selection that varies in color, shape, texture, and size.

2) After making a symmetrical design, experiment with asymmetrical patterns.

PROJECT TWO: PIN

MATERIALS

campaign button or cardboard and pin back • glue • beads with flat sides • clear nail polish • acrylic paint (optional) • tweezers (optional)

DIRECTIONS

1. Paint the surface of the button or cardboard if it is not a solid color. Allow the paint to dry.

2. Glue the beads to the button or cardboard. (If the beads are small, use a pair of tweezers to pick them up.) Allow the glue to dry.

3. Cover the surface with clear nail polish.

TIP: Although small beads allow for a more detailed design, they should be used by older students only. Large beads are far easier for young students to handle.

POTTERY DESIGNS

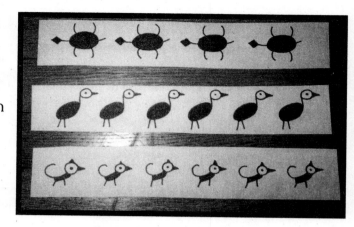

The ancient Hohokams were accomplished potters. On many of their works, they painted red patterns of geometric designs and animal shapes against the natural buff color of the clay. On some pieces, however, they reversed the red-on-buff color scheme by making use of a resist process. In this technique, Hohokams first painted designs on pots with wax. They then coated the uncovered areas with red pigment. When the pots were fired, the wax burned off, leaving the unpainted clay visible in the spots where the wax had been.

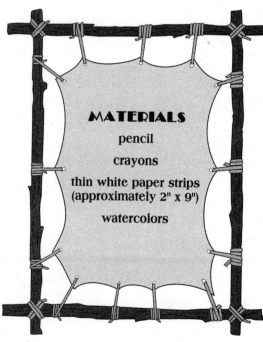

MATERIALS

pencil

crayons

thin white paper strips
(approximately 2" x 9")

watercolors

DIRECTIONS

1. Using a pencil, on a white paper strip create animal designs using basic geometric shapes, such as rectangles, ovals, triangles, circles, and diamonds. If you want design ideas, turn to the petroglyph patterns on page 75.

2. Trace over your animal designs with a dark-colored crayon.

3. Color in the animal outlines until each animal is coated thickly with crayon wax.

4. Paint the strip with watercolor paint. The wax of the crayon will resist the paint, so only the background of the drawings will take its color.

5. Your pottery designs are done! Use these strips to decorate jars and cans, or display them on your classroom wall.

CRADLEBOARD

Many Native American groups, including the Mojaves of Arizona, carried their babies on cradleboards. Wrapped in blankets or skins, infants were tied snugly to these boards, which were fitted with straps so parents could wear them on their backs or attach them to the side of a horse. Mothers sometimes used twine to hang cradleboards between two trees like a hammock so they could look after their babies while they performed their daily work.

To protect the baby's head and provide shade from the desert sun, a woven reed hoop was affixed near the top of Mojave cradleboards. Often brightly colored beaded balls and baubles called dream-catcher hoops were strung from it like mobiles.

DIRECTIONS

1. Glue three popsicle sticks to the paper. Draw a baby's face on a fourth stick.

2. Cut out a 1/3" x 3" rectangle from oaktag. Draw lines on it to imitate weaving. (Bend the ends in and glue them to the back of the glued sticks as the hoop that comes forward in front of the baby's face.)

3. Place the baby on the cradleboard, and wrap the fabric around the baby and the cradleboard. Tie the baby and blanket in place with yarn.

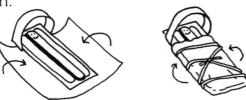

4. Draw a dream-catcher hoop and a brightly colored ball on oaktag, and cut them out.

5. Thread a needle, and knot the end of the thread. Run the needle first through the top of the ball, then through the hoop above the baby's head, leaving a length of thread between them. Tie a knot, and cut off the excess thread. (Do the same to suspend the dream-catcher hoop.)

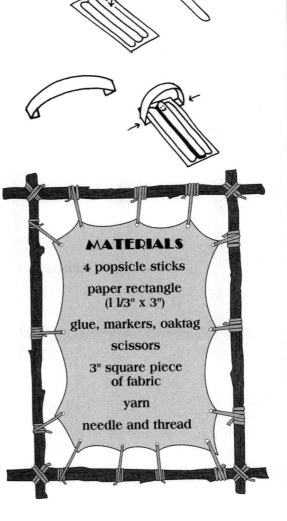

MATERIALS

4 popsicle sticks

paper rectangle (1 1/3" x 3")

glue, markers, oaktag

scissors

3" square piece of fabric

yarn

needle and thread

HOGAN

The largest Indian tribe in the United States, the Navajos traditionally lived in one-family dwellings known as hogans (the Navajo word for "home place"). Hogans usually had six or eight walls built from logs and covered with bark, leaves, or animal skins. For insulation, the exterior was coated with mud and dirt. A hole was left in one of the house's walls to serve as a door. The door always faced the east, so that each morning the family could pay its respects to the rising sun.

According to the Blessingway Myth, which tells the story of the Navajos' creation, the tribe learned how to make hogans from a deity named Talking God. Talking God also told the Navajos that hogans were alive and must be cared for in special ways. After a hogan was constructed, oak sprigs were stuffed between the logs of the roof, and corn pollen was sprinkled toward the north, south, east, and west. The male head of the household sang one of the hundreds of Navajo house-blessing songs to ensure that the dwellings' inhabitants would live in beauty and harmony.

MATERIALS

garden clippers

popsicle sticks

cardboard base
(9" x 11")

glue

clay

small rocks

straw or dried grass

sand

DIRECTIONS

1. Using garden clippers, cut up a few popsicle sticks into small pieces. Glue a piece to one end of several popsicle sticks, and set them aside. (You may want to prepare these sticks in advance.)

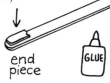

end piece

GLUE

2. Glue one regular popsicle stick in the middle of each side of the cardboard.

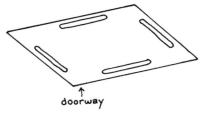

doorway

3. Connect the sticks on the cardboard base by gluing sticks diagonally on top. See diagram at right. Don't forget to designate one corner as the doorway. (Do not place any sticks here.)

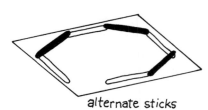

alternate sticks

4. Glue a popsicle stick on top of each of the four sticks placed in place in Step 2. For the sides near the open doorway corner, use one of the sticks prepared in Step 1. The end with the extra piece attached should be glued by the doorway.

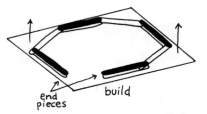

5. Repeat Step 3 and Step 4. Continue alternating between these steps until the walls on your model are about 4" high.

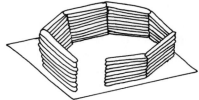

6. Make one layer of seven popsicle sticks (two vertical, two horizontal, and three diagonal). This will be the base of the structure's roof; if you want a removable roof, do not glue this layer to the model.

7. Build up the domed roof by gluing on layers of sticks to the base. You will want to make your shape gets smaller and smaller as you reach the top. Sticks may be glued at an angle to best cover the space.

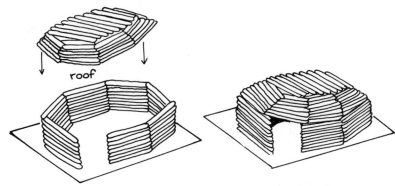

8. Press moist clay into some of the openings on the model's sides. Then, press small rocks and straw or grass into the clay.

9. Apply glue to the roof and cardboard base, and sprinkle the glue with sand. Glue a little sand, here and there, on the sides.

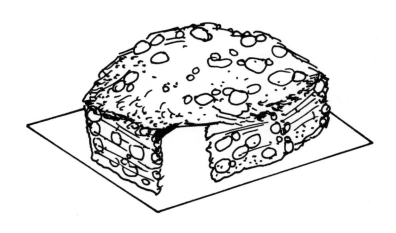

SILVER WORK

In the late nineteenth century, Navajo men were introduced to silversmithing. Their teachers were Mexican craftsmen, who were brought to the Navajo reservation by non-Indian traders. These traders had created a lucrative business out of selling Navajo artwork, particularly their beautiful woven blankets and rugs, to tourists from the East. They hoped that Navajo silversmiths could provide them with more goods to satisfy the growing demands of their customers. Almost immediately, the Navajos became master smiths, accomplished in making a wide variety of wares, including belt buckles, buttons, bracelets, rings, necklaces, and horse bridles.

The first project below is inspired by a Navajo pendant that was made in 1994. It was formed from two silver circles that were hammered over a round mold. In addition to shaping the circles into bowls, the hammering produced an irregular surface that shimmers as it reflects light. Line designs were then stamped into the discs with a pointed tool and a hammer, and two were soldered together to form a hollow bead. The second project borrows the design of a Navajo silver pin dating from the 1880s. The shape of the base is a rectangle with wavy edges. At its center is an oval, surrounded by leaflike shapes and etched line designs.

MATERIALS

clay

pointed tool

string

silver paint and brush
or foil and glue

chain, cord, or yarn

PROJECT ONE: NECKLACE WITH SILVER ORNAMENT

DIRECTIONS

1. Roll a small ball out of clay.

2. Using the pointed tool, poke a hole through the center to form a large clay bead.

3. Draw a line design around the hole on each side with the pointed tool. (For example, you may draw a flower with the hole as its center.) Make the lines fairly deep.

4. Place the bead on a piece of string, and paint the bead silver. Hang it up to dry.

5. Remove the bead, and discard the string. If you don't wish to use paint, cover the bead first with glue and then with foil, turning the foil ends inside the holes in the bead. Allow the glue to dry.

6. String the bead on a chain, cord, or piece of yarn.

PROJECT TWO: DECORATED BOX

MATERIALS

box (with lid) • clay • black acrylic paint • pointed tool • plastic knife • oaktag • foil • glue • scissors

DIRECTIONS

1. Paint the box, and set it aside to dry.

2. Cut a piece of oaktag the size of the box lid. Then place a slab of clay about 1/4" thick on the oaktag base. Use a plastic knife to cut wavy lines around the edges.

clay slab

3. Make another slab of clay about 1/4" thick. (Using a pointed tool or toothpick, draw an oval and leaflike shapes on the slab, and cut them out with the plastic knife.) Place the shapes on the clay base to check that all will fit. Take the clay shapes off the base, and allow them to dry.

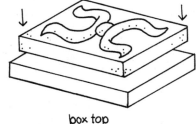

box top

4. Place the shapes and the base on foil, and cut out enough foil to cover each.

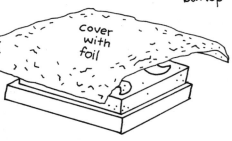

cover with foil

5. Apply glue over the surface of each clay shape and the clay base, and place the foil pieces on top.

6. Wrap the foil edges under the shapes. Glue the shapes to the clay base, and then glue the clay base is to the top of the box. Dry.

TIPS:

1) Plasticine can be used instead of clay, but the result will not be as durable.

2) Some students may have difficulty drawing a leaf shape. To make a large leaf, they can instead form a coil of clay, place it on a flat surface in the shape of an S, and then round the edges. For smaller leaves, they can mold a diamond from a pinch of clay and, again, round the edges.

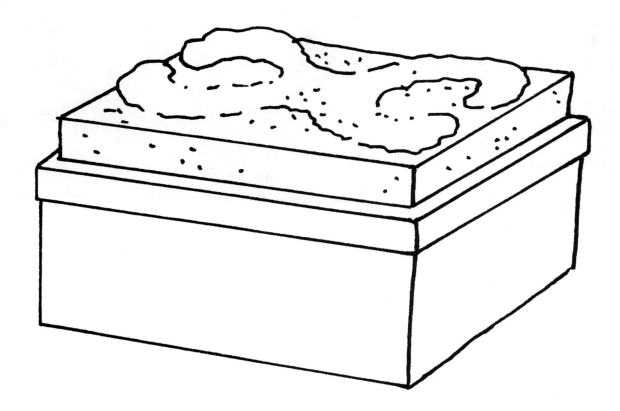

WEARING BLANKET

Spanish explorers brought sheep to the Navajo homeland in about 1600. Initially, the Navajos raised sheep for meat, but soon they came to value the animals for their wool as well. By the end of the seventeenth century, their Pueblo neighbors had taught them how to spin the wool and weave the yarn on large upright looms to make beautiful blankets, which the Navajos took to wearing around their shoulders like cloaks. Navajo women quickly became expert weavers. According to Navajo legend, this talent was a gift from Spider Woman, whose own loom was the sky.

Following the example of their Pueblo teachers, the Navajos' first blankets were patterned with stripes of white, black, and brown, the natural colors of sheep wool. In time, they learned to color their yarn using pigments they made from vegetables and minerals. At the beginning of the 19th century, they began to trade with non-Indians for yarn that had been colored with commercial dyes. These bright dyes appealed to the Navajos; they particularly favored red, which became the dominant color used in many of these blankets. Excited by their new palette, Navajo weavers started experimenting with different patterns featuring zigzags, diamond shapes, and thick and narrow bands in a wide variety of combinations.

MATERIALS

large white paper

red and black crayons

black marker

cardboard

PROJECT ONE: POSTER ONE

DIRECTIONS

1. On a white sheet of paper make a symmetrical design using zigzags, squares, and triangles. (Or use the pattern on page 63.)

2. Color the areas red and black. Leave some of the areas white.

3. Mount your design on a piece of cardboard and display!

PROJECT TWO: GRAPH PAPER DESIGN

MATERIALS

graph paper • pencil • markers

DIRECTIONS

1. Plan design starting in the middle. (Plan one unit to be white, two units to be red and several units to be black. Then two red and one white at the bottom.

2. Work to the right and the left with matching stripes that are red and then black, both descending in lengths. White areas will all be two units on the end after the central one.)

TIP: When plotting the design, place a dot in each square to remind you what color it should be.

PROJECT THREE: CUT-PAPER PLACE MAT

MATERIALS

colored paper • marker • ruler • scissors • glue • clear contact paper

DIRECTIONS

1. Make a grid on red paper. (Cut out a step-diamond shape.)

2. Cut black strips (one long and then sets of descending lengths) and glue stripes in place.

3. Glue red step design on black background.

4. Cover with contact paper.

RUG

In the late 1860s, Navajo women first began using their weaving skill to create rugs. They were given the idea by traders, who knew rugs would sell better to their non-Indian clientele than the woven blankets Navajo weavers traditionally made for use by their families.

As they were learning to make rugs, the Navajos obtained new materials, such as chemical-based dyes and commercial wool, which inspired them to develop new designs. One of their favorite patterns of the period—a collection of vertical lines surrounding a central motif, usually a serrated or saw-toothed diamond shape—was featured on many of the earliest Navajo rugs.

DIRECTIONS

1. Cut 1-inch strips of red, black and white paper as indicated on the diagram on the following page.

2. Glue the 11"-long red strip horizontally in the middle of the black piece of paper. Measure to make sure that there is 7" of black paper above and below the red strip.

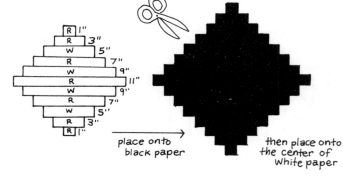

place onto black paper

then place onto the center of white paper

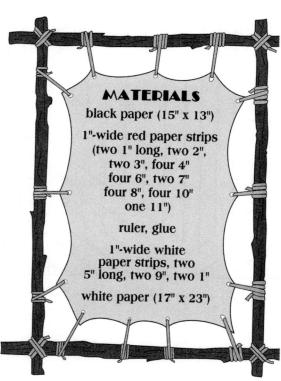

MATERIALS

black paper (15" x 13")

1"-wide red paper strips (two 1" long, two 2", two 3", four 4" four 6", two 7" four 8", four 10" one 11")

ruler, glue

1"-wide white paper strips, two 5" long, two 9", two 1"

white paper (17" x 23")

3. Glue 9" white strips on each side of the 11" red strip. Continue gluing red and white strips onto the black paper as shown in the diagram.

4. When you complete the pattern, cut the black paper creating a 1/2" border around the red and white strips.

5. Glue the black step design in the middle of the white paper, measuring to be sure there is 1" on the top and 2" on the sides.

6. Glue 10" red strips in the corners of the white paper.

7. Leave a 2" white space and glue 8", 6", 4", and 2" red strips in place to complete the design.

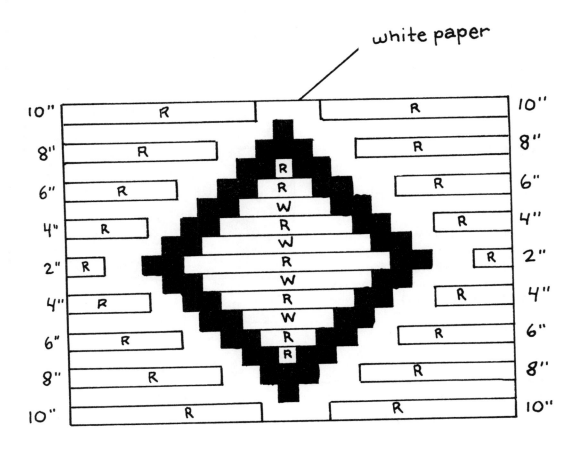

white paper

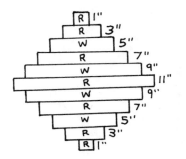

WEAVING DESIGNS

The patterns on Navajo rugs and blankets are generally made up of only stripes and basic geometric shapes. However, by placing certain colors and shapes side-by-side, Navajo weavers often create dazzling effects with these simple elements. For instance, they frequently juxtapose bright complementary colors or colors of very different values. In these combinations, the colors become so vivid they seem to vibrate.

DIRECTIONS

1. Make a wide black zigzag line down the center of a large piece of yellow paper.

2. Leaving a space of yellow next to the black line, make red, orange, and black zigzags on each side. Use the colors in the following order until the paper is covered: red, orange, black, orange, red.

TRY THIS:

1. Use the patterns on the following page to recreate other dazzling designs!

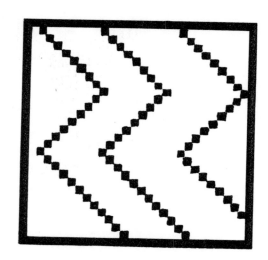

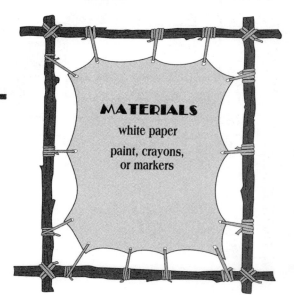

MATERIALS

white paper

paint, crayons, or markers

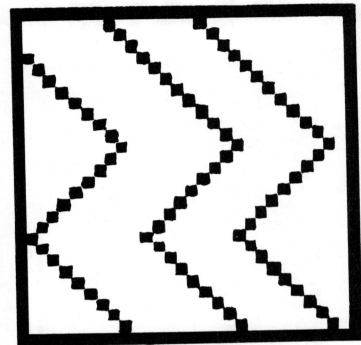

EYE DAZZLER

TRADITIONAL

WEARING

STAR

PUEBLO VILLAGE

In 1540, when the Spanish arrived in the American Southwest, they were greatly impressed by the huge housing complexes they came upon in the villages of the Indians of what is now New Mexico. These dwellings were like large multistoried apartment buildings made of bricks of adobe (sun-dried clay). The Spanish called these buildings "pueblos," the Spanish word for "city" or "town." (They also gave this name to all the Indians who lived in this type of dwelling, even though these peoples belonged to several different, distinct tribes. The Indians now known as the Pueblos include groups such as the Zunis, Hopis, Acomas, and Tewas.)

The earliest pueblos had only one opening—a hole in the roof accessible with a ladder that served as an entrance. After contact with Europeans, the Pueblos began to add doors at the ground level and windows to the buildings' sides. The height of the various dwellings was staggered so that the roof of one functioned as a exterior work space for the inhabitants of the dwelling above. In this exterior space, the Pueblos performed various chores, such as tanning animal hides and making pottery.

PROJECT ONE:
PUEBLO VILLAGE CLASS MODEL

MATERIALS

boxes of
various sizes

scissors

tan paint

marker

DIRECTIONS

1. As a class, decide whether you want to make an early or late pueblo design. For an early pueblo, cut a hole in the top of one box to serve as an entrance. For a late pueblo, cut out doors and windows from several boxes.

2. Arrange boxes so that doors open to rooftop work areas. Glue the boxes together, and dry.

3. Paint the model tan, and dry.

PROJECT TWO: MINIATURES FOR PUEBLO VILLAGE

SKIN-DRYING RACK

DIRECTIONS

(Stick frames for drying felt skins. Glue popsicle sticks together. Dry. Cut out animal skin shapes from tan felt, and glue to stick frames.)

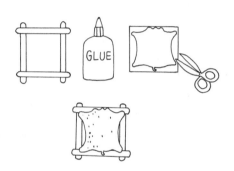

MATERIALS

popsicle sticks, toothpicks

scissors, glue

tan felt, twigs

clay, pencil

yellow, orange, red cellophane

needle, heavy thread

clothespins

macoroni shell (smallest available)

COOKING FRAME AND FIRE

DIRECTIONS

1. Glue three popsicle sticks together to form a U-shape. Dry.

2. Place ends of the U in clay, so that the frame stands upright.

3. Glue a pile of small twigs together. Cut the edges of cellophane into flamelike shapes, and glue them to the twigs.

4. Place the cooking frame over the fire.

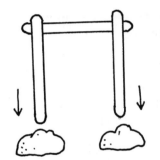

clay

TALL HANGING POT

DIRECTIONS

1. Make a tall pot with a rounded bottom, forming the clay around the eraser end of the pencil. Remove the pencil.

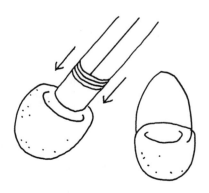

2. Sew through the pot with a needle and thread while the clay is still moist. Knot the ends of the thread to make a hanger.

3. Etch a design around the edge of the pot mouth with a toothpick.

INDIVIDUAL BOWLS AND SPOONS

DIRECTIONS

1. Make individual bowls from balls of clay, pressed on top with a pencil eraser to make a hole.

2. Glue toothpicks to mini-macaroni shells to make spoons. For added durability, place an additional drop of glue on the point at which each shell and toothpick meet. Allow the glue to dry.

TIPS:

1) Encourage students to use the model and clothespin people and horses to reenact stories about the Pueblos. Playing with the model in this way can provide the basis for writing lessons or inspire students to do additional research and make new miniatures. (For more information, read *Growing Up Indian* by Evelyn Wolfson and *Native Americans* by Mary Strohl and Susan Schneck.)

2) If you choose not to keep it in your display at the end of the year, hold a drawing to select a student to take it home or donate it to a local library for display.

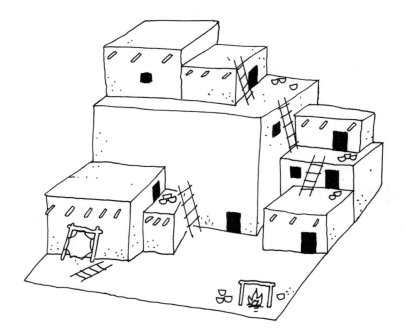

CLAY TURTLE SCULPTURE

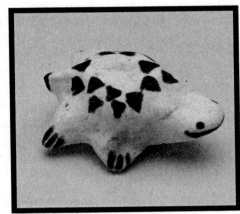

The ancient Mogollon and Hohokam peoples of the Southwest made small, simple sculptures of animals out of clay. They added details to these stylized figurines with paint and incised lines. The project below is based on a white clay sculpture made in 1992 by an Acoma Pueblo artist following in the tradition of these early Southwestern Indian artisans. This tiny turtle effigy is only 2 3/4" long and decorated with black paint and pressed designs.

DIRECTIONS

1. Make a ball out of clay, and flatten it. Pinch one side to form the turtle's head, or attach a piece of clay for the head, and blend it into the body so that no line shows between the two pieces.

2. Pinch the opposite end of the body to make a little tail. Pinch clay from the sides or add clay and blend to make legs.

3. Using a pointed tool, sketch two circles on the back of the turtle. (The exterior circle will mark the points of the star. The interior circle will remain blank.)

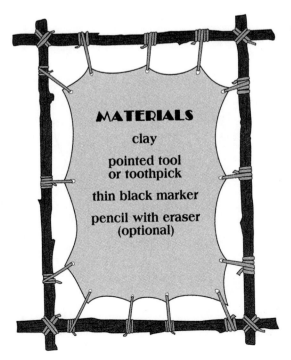

MATERIALS

clay

pointed tool
or toothpick

thin black marker

pencil with eraser
(optional)

4. Use the eraser to press marks into the back of the turtle. (First outline the interior circle with indented eraser marks. Then decrease the number of the indented markings to achieve the points to form a star.) (If you prefer, you can make the triangle star design with the marker on dry clay.)

5. Allow the clay to dry, and draw details with the marker.

CORN DESIGN

By developing methods of farming using very little water, the Hopis were able to grow a variety of crops in the dry, sandy soil of their homeland. They cultivated beans, squash, cotton, and tobacco, but their most versatile crop was corn. The Hopis had more than 50 ways of preparing corn, making it the staple of their diet.

In 1983, artist Iris Nampeyo celebrated the importance of this food to her people by creating a beautiful pottery jar in the shape of an ear of corn. This work is the inspiration for the projects below. Iris Nampeyo is a descendant of the famed Hopi potter Nampeyo (1856–1942), whose pottery revived many designs of the Hopis' ancestors, the prehistoric Anasazis.

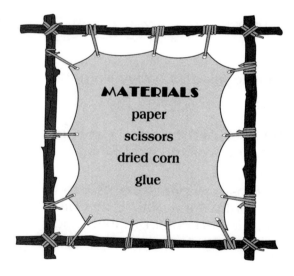

MATERIALS

paper

scissors

dried corn

glue

PROJECT ONE: CORN COLLAGE

DIRECTIONS

1. Cut an interesting shape out of paper to use as a background.

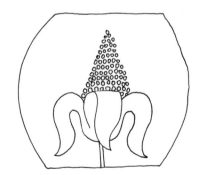

2. Glue corn to paper in a tall triangular formation.

3. Cut green stem and leaves) and glue to them to the bottom of the corn triangle. (Glue one side of the leaves to the paper; leave the other side free so that the leaves extend in relief.)

PROJECT TWO: CORN PLAQUE

MATERIALS

clay • plastic knife or round-ended tool • pointed tool

DIRECTIONS

1. Form an oval-shaped slab of clay with round edges.

2. Press the plastic knife into the clay, making indentions that resemble kernels.

3. Form a stem and leaves from clay. Attach the stem and the bases of the leaves to the bottom of the slab.

4. Secure one side of each leaf to the slab. Move other side forward to create a three-dimensional effect.

5. Make two holes at the top of the sculpture with the pointed tool. Allow it to dry, and hang.

PETROGLYPHS

Some of the first Indian artists used boulders and cave walls as their canvases. In addition to painting these surfaces with designs made with vegetable and mineral pigments, they scraped away the top layer of the rock to make incised images now known as petroglyphs. Some petroglyphs are figures of humans and animals, often drawn in silhouette. These drawings were probably meant to record events in the lives of the artists or in the history of their people. Others are seemingly abstract designs; these were possibly religious symbols.

Although time and the elements have destroyed many of the earliest Indian petroglyphs, some have been discovered on rock faces and in caves throughout North America. Many of the best preserved have been found in the lands of Pueblo groups, such as the Tewas and the Hopis.

PROJECT ONE: PETROGLYPH MURAL

DIRECTIONS

1. Tack mural paper to a bulletin board.

2. As a class, cover the paper with petroglyphs using markers or crayons. Use the patterns on the opposite page for ideas.

3. Take down the mural. Cut it up into puzzle-like pieces for the class to reassemble or into sections for the students to take home.

MATERIALS

mural paper

tacks

markers
or crayons

BASKET

Basketry is one of the oldest arts practiced by humans. Some 1,500 years ago, the Pueblos' ancestors, the Anasazis, were already master basketmakers. The modern Zuni Indians inherited much of their knowledge of basketry techniques from these ancient people.

Carefully weaving together contrasting colors, the Zunis create a variety of geometric shapes on their baskets. Among the most common Zuni design motifs are zigzags, dots, bars, triangles, and abstract leaflike designs.

DIRECTIONS

1. Place one bag inside the other.

2. Roll the top of the bags down and out.

3. Paint horizontal bands of white and red around the exterior, and allow the paint to dry.

4. Draw line designs on the outside with the marker.

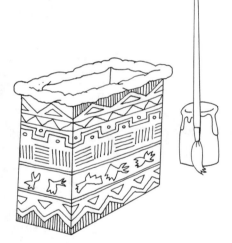

MATERIALS

two large paper bags

red and white acrylic paint

thick black marker

TIP: Coating the inside and outside of the bags with acrylic paint makes these baskets so sturdy they can be used for many years.

DOLLS

Yuma artisans are well known for their hand-modeled clay dolls, which they clothed and decorated with scraps of fabric, glass beads, and horsehair. Most of these charming figurines were made during the late nineteenth and early twentieth centuries for sale to non-Indian tourists. However, they harken back to earlier Indian traditions. The colorful designs on the dolls' bodies were painted with the same pigments and patterns that the Yumas traditionally used to adorn themselves for ceremonial dances. The dolls also resemble artifacts made by the Hohokam people, who lived near the Yumas' southwestern Arizona homeland for thousands of years.

DIRECTIONS

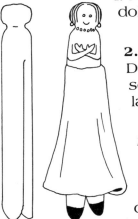

1. Make a male and a female doll out of clay or clothespins.

2. With markers, draw the faces and, if using clothespins, arms. Darken the hair areas. Add dots around the dolls' necks to represent a bead necklace. (If you prefer, make the dolls a tiny necklace by stringing seed beads with needle and thread.)

3. Glue on beads for earrings. Make a skirt for the female by wrapping a piece of felt around the doll's waist and overlapping it in the front. (Add stitches down the front of the skirt if desired.) Cut two 1" squares of felt, and glue them to the front and back of the male doll to make a loincloth.

4. Form a small ball of clay. Flatten the ball on one side, and press a pencil eraser into the other side to create a miniature pot.

5. Turn pot upside down, and glue it to the top of the female doll's head. Allow the glue to dry. Add designs to the pot with markers.

MATERIALS

clay or clothespins

thin-point markers

glue, seed beads

felt, scissors

pencil with new eraser

needle and thread (optional)

California Great Basin Plateau

MAN'S PURSE

Shells were used by many Indians as ornaments, but to some groups they had an additional value. For instance, along much of the Pacific coast, dentalia shells functioned as a medium of exchange. Dentalia were the small white shells of mollusks native to the western shore of Canada's Vancouver Island. Northwest Coast Indians collected the delicate shells, strung them together, and traded them to Indians living from as far north as Alaska to as far south as California. These Indians then used the shells as money when trading with one another.

The men of the Hupa tribe of northwestern California fashioned unique purses to carry their dentalia strings. These purses were made by plugging up the ends of an elk antler and cutting a slot in its side. The shells were slipped into the slot, which was then covered with a piece of buckskin held in place with a thong. Some Hupas decorated their purses by etching a line design into the antler and rubbing it with charcoal to blacken the incised lines.

DIRECTIONS

1. Trace the circle end of the cylinder on paper, and draw a circle around it with a diameter 1/2" larger than that of the first. Cut out the larger circle, and use it to trace and cut out a second one.

2. Tape one circle to each end of the cylinder.

MATERIALS

cardboard cylinder

pencil, white paper

scissors

masking tape

markers, oaktag

glue

rawhide shoelace
or yarn

3. Cut a slit in the cylinder with sharp scissors. (Teachers may want to help students with this step.) Using markers, decorate the cylinder with lines, triangles, and zigzags.

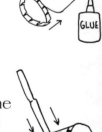

4. Cut a rectangle of oaktag that is longer and wider than the slit. Glue on the rawhide or a piece of yarn to use as a tie.

5. Place the oaktag over the slit, and hold it in place by tying the rawhide or yarn around the cylinder.

MAT HOUSE

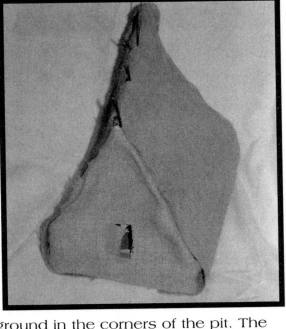

The Nez Perce´ Indians lived in what is now central Idaho and portions of Washington and Oregon. With the changing seasons, they moved throughout this large territory, traveling to whatever location offered them the greatest sources of fish, game, or wild plant foods. While tracking animals during the summer hunting season or harvesting salmon during their annual spring runs, the Nez Perce´s inhabited temporary tipilike shelters. But when the weather turned cold, they retreated to their permanent villages, which consisted of five or six mat houses. Measuring from 25 to 60 feet long, each of these large dwellings housed several families.

When building a mat house, the Nez Perce´ first dug a rectangular pit about two feet deep. Four forked poles were set in the ground in the corners of the pit. The tops of the poles were then brought together in the center, over which a long ridge pole was laid. To complete the frame, more poles were added to the structure's sides, which then were covered with overlapping mats made from various types of reeds and grasses.

DIRECTIONS

1. Tape a twig to each of the four corners of the box lid. Use 3" lengths of tape, first wrapping them around the twigs and then attaching them to the ends of the box. (Take care to attach the twigs firmly.)

2. Pull the top of the twigs together toward the center, creating a triangular shape at both sides of the box.

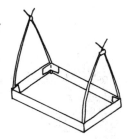

MATERIALS

shoe box lid

12"-long twigs
(preferably forked)

masking tape

ruler

burlap

scissors

sand or dirt

3. Place a twig across the top, then add another triangle at the center of the lid. This is the frame of your mat house.

4. Measure and cut the burlap to cover your frame and about 1" at the bottom of each side of the lid, as shown. Make three holes at the top to fit the twigs that stick out. Fold the burlap in half, and stick the twigs through the center of the burlap.

5. Tape the ends of the burlap under the box.

6. Cut triangular pieces of burlap to fit the sides.

7. Cut a small door in the side of the fabric, just above the box edge.

8. Pour sand or dirt around the model's outside edge up to the height of the shoe box to create the impression that the interior is 2' underground. (Placing the model in a large shallow box before pouring will keep the sand or dirt from spilling on the floor.)

9. Remove any tape that shows.

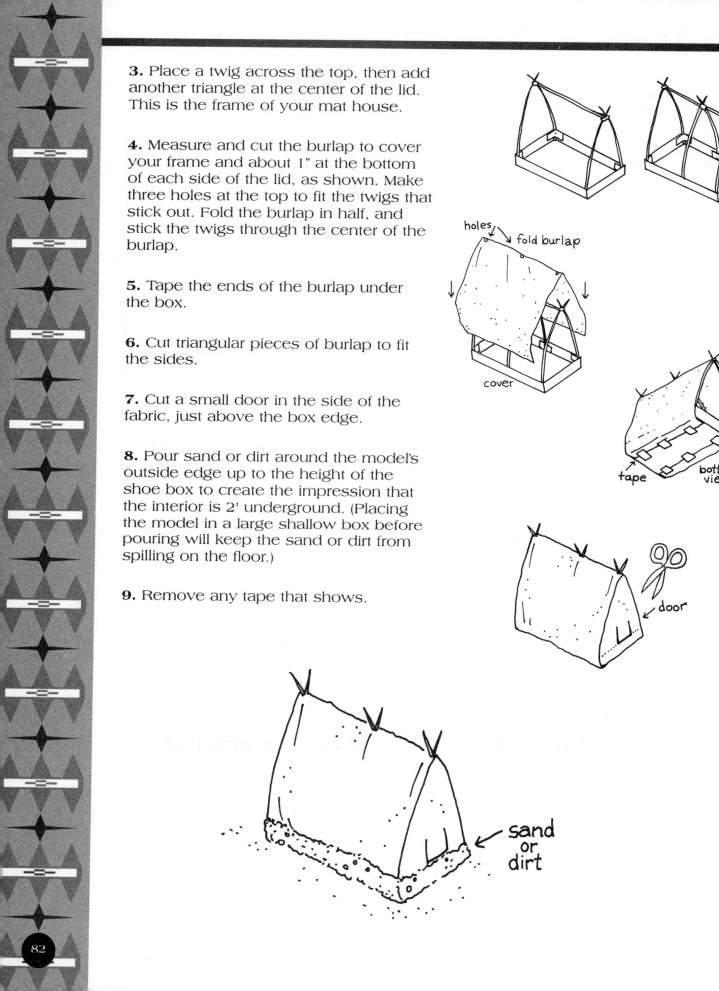

SHELTER

Native to the grassy river valleys of what is now central California, the Pomos took full advantage of the rich plant life that flourished in their territory. They gathered reeds, roots, and tree bark, and expertly wove them to create almost everything they needed, including baskets, clothing, and boats. The Pomos also used these materials to build their homes.

Because of the warm climate of their territory, the tribe's housing needs were minimal. Pomo dwellings were little more than a brush roof tied to the top of poles set into the ground. These simple shelters provided shade from the sun and protection from rain.

DIRECTIONS

1. Place 3 sticks (or straws) in a U formation, and tape their ends together. Repeat to form a second U.

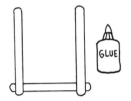

2. Make four clay balls. Place the ends of two U's into the clay balls, so that the U's stand upright.

3. Tape two more sticks to the top of the U's, forming a rectangle.

MATERIALS

8 sticks or drinking straws

masking tape

clay

oaktag

straw or dried grass

4. Turn the rectangle roof over, and tape it to a piece of oaktag slightly larger than the rectangle.

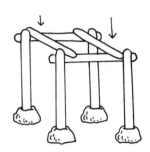

oak tag

tape

5. Stand the frame upright, and glue straw or grass to the roof.

grass or straw

DANCE WANDS

Inhabitants of the desert lands between the Rocky Mountains and the Sierra Nevadas, the Shoshones performed elaborate religious rituals to celebrate and seek the protection of supernatural beings. Dancing was central to these lengthy ceremonies. Sometimes, a dance was performed over as many as four nights and three days.

The Shoshones treasured the special objects they made for use during these dances. They adorned them with every type of decorative ornament and technique at their disposal—including intricate quillwork and beadwork, feathers in all shapes and sizes, and colorful ribbons, yarn, and cloth. Many of these elements were combined in their elaborate dance wands, which dancers waved while they performed. Often attached to dance wands were streams of satin ribbons, yarn tassels, and strands of glass beads that shimmered in the firelight or strings of metal janglers that jingled as gently or as wildly as the dancer moved.

The projects below are based on two Shoshone dance wands made in the early twentieth century. The first featured a painted red stick decorated with quillwork circles, from which elaborately cut feathers radiated. The second was made from a forked twig adorned with bands of small colorful seed beads, quilled tassels with tin janglers, dyed horsehair, and eagle tail feathers.

MATERIALS

oaktag or paper
(9"x 12" piece)

compass

scissors

glue

stick

red
construction paper

yarn

PROJECT ONE: DANCE WAND WITH QUILLWORK DECORATION

DIRECTIONS

1. Cut a 9" circle out of oaktag. Draw a small circle on the scrap of leftover oaktag, and cut it out. Place the smaller circle in the center of the larger one, and trace around it. Then draw an x through the two smaller circles, and decorate them with lines of color to imitate quillwork.

2. Make four evenly spaced cuts into the 9" circle, stopping at the center circle. Carefully continue making cuts around the larger circle, feathering its edges.

3. Cut out several 1/4"-wide strips of varying lengths from the remaining oaktag. Glue the strips to the back of the 9" circle so they radiate in all directions.

4. Tape the end of the stick to the back of the 9" circle, and staple the small circle to the stick.

5. Cut several small triangles out of red construction paper. Lay the wand on a flat surface, and dot the longer strips with glue. Place the triangles over the dots.

6. Tie yarn (under the radiating design) so that it dangles below.

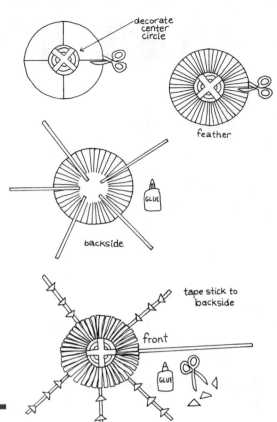

TIP: If desired, before beginning the project, paint the stick red with acrylic paint, and allow it to dry.

PROJECT TWO: DANCE WAND WITH TASSEL, FEATHERS, AND STREAMERS

MATERIALS

acrylic paint • forked stick • yarn • cardboard (2"-wide piece) • feathers • silver streamers (or tinsel or strips of aluminum foil)

DIRECTIONS

1. Paint the stick with bands of color, and allow it to dry.

2. Repeatedly wrap the yarn around the piece of cardboard. Tie the yarn on one end of the cardboard. Snip the yarn at the other end, and tie a piece of yarn around the cut pieces to create a tassel.

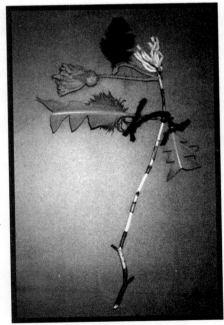

3. Tie feathers, pieces of yarn, silver streamers, and the tassel to the end of the stick.

MAT HOUSE

The Yokuts, who lived in central California's San Joaquin river valley, used tule—the leaves of bulrush plant— as their primary building material. In October, they collected tule from the bulrushes that grew wild in the swampy areas of their homeland. After allowing the leaves to dry, they fashioned them into mats woven so tightly that they were waterproof. The mats were then placed in over-lapping rows over a wedge-shaped wooden frame to create dwellings large enough to house several families. In most Yokut villages, these mat houses were built in a row, with the chief's house in the middle. Outside the houses stood an enormous mat-covered arbor that shaded the entire village from the sun.

DIRECTIONS

1. Cut two cardboard rectangles measuring 5" x 6". Line up the cardboard pieces side by side on a flat surface with the 6" sides touching. Tape them together, turn them over, and tape the other side for added strength. This is your dwelling's roof.

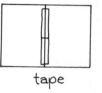

tape

2. Bend the roof along the tape to create a triangle. Place the roof on its side (triangular-edge down) on a piece of cardboard, lining up the base with the edge of the cardboard. Using a pencil, draw around the sides of the roof, producing a triangle on the cardboard.

fold

trace then cut

3. Cut out the triangle. Trace and cut out a second triangle out of cardboard.

4. Place one of the triangles on a flat surface, and put the roof, triangular-edge down, over it. Tape the edges where the two pieces meet on the inside.

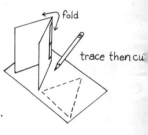

tape inside

5. Cut a door.

MATERIALS
cardboard
scissors
masking tape
pencil, glue
dried grass
or straw

6. Apply glue to all the outside surfaces of the model, and attach the dried grass or straw. Allow the glue to dry. Repeat the process to add more grass or straw to areas that are not completely covered.

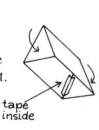

doorway

Northwest Coast

THUNDERBIRD HOUSE SCULPTURE

The entrances of the houses of Northwest Coast Indians were often decorated with paintings or sculptures of animal spirits. Many of these artworks were visual reminders of the myths about these supernatural beings. For instance, one dwelling in a Bella Coola village was topped with an enormous wooden thunderbird. The thunderbird was a symbol of the sky, or upper world. On many house paintings, a thunderbird is pictured above a whale, an image that represents the dominance of the upper world over the underworld, the whale's ocean domain.

DIRECTIONS

1. Place two popsicle sticks vertically, one above the other, on a flat surface. They will be the head and part of the tail of your thunderbird.

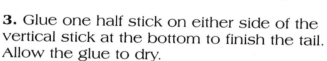

2. Glue two sticks horizontally on top of the others to form the body.

3. Glue one half stick on either side of the vertical stick at the bottom to finish the tail. Allow the glue to dry.

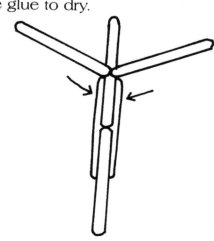

MATERIALS

popsicle sticks
(cut some in half
with sharp scissors
or garder clippers
in advance

glue
(place in freezer
to make thicker

markers

4. Turn your work over. On both sides, glue a stick extending (at an angle) from the top of the two body sticks. These will be the top of the wings.

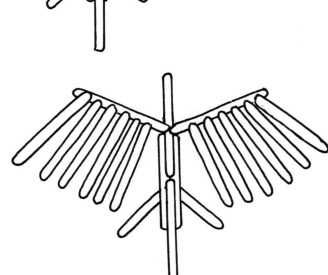

5. Below the top wing stick, glue as many sticks as will comfortably fit (3–6) to create the wing feathers. Dry.

6. Draw eyes and a diamond-shaped bill on the thunderbird's head.

TIP: Be sure to allow enough time for the glue to dry completely between steps. While waiting, students can write their own stories about Northwest Coast animal spirits, such as Thunderbird, Whale, Eagle, and Raven.

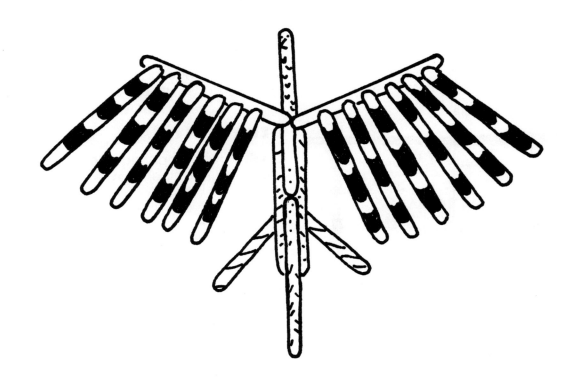

Miniature Totem Pole

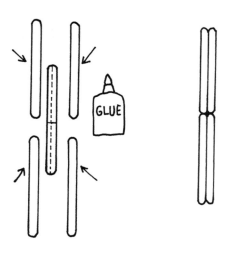

Northwest Coast Indian artists made a wide array of beautiful objects. But their most well known and grandest works were their totem poles. These enormous sculptures, made from tree trunks, stood as high as 50 feet and were decorated with elaborate carvings of people, animals, and supernatural beings. They were erected outside the houses of important families, who believed they were granted their wealth and power from an animal spirit ancestor. Like a coat of arms, the carvings on a family's totem pole were a pictorial family history. They told the story of its spirit ancestor and celebrated the heroic exploits of family members past and present. Therefore, erecting a totem pole allowed a family both to pay respect to the spirit world and to remind their neighbors of their powerful position in the village.

Seeing how much totem poles impressed non-Indian visitors to the Northwest, Indian craftspeople began to make miniature versions for sale to tourists. The most distinctive miniatures were created by the Haidas. Instead of wood, they carved their small totem poles out of argillite, a dark black stone. So soft it can be cut with woodworking tools, argillite is mined only on the Haidas' homeland on Queen Charlotte Island, located off the coast of British Columbia.

MATERIALS

popsicle sticks

glue

markers

clay

DIRECTIONS

1. Glue four popsicle sticks onto one stick as shown.

GLUE

2. Join sticks by gluing a fifth stick across all four ends as shown. Dry flat.

3. Use markers to draw animals on the sticks.

4. Make a clay ball, flatten it on the bottom, and insert the pole into the clay. Pinch the clay around the sticks, so that the pole is well rooted and freestanding.

TIP: This method is quick, easy, and neat. However, if you prefer a three-dimensional totem pole, you can also make this project with modeling clay.

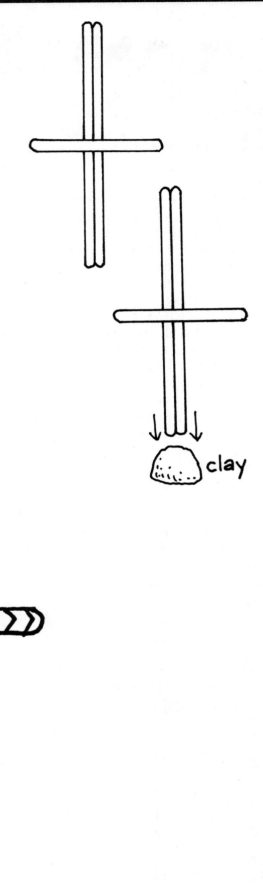

clay

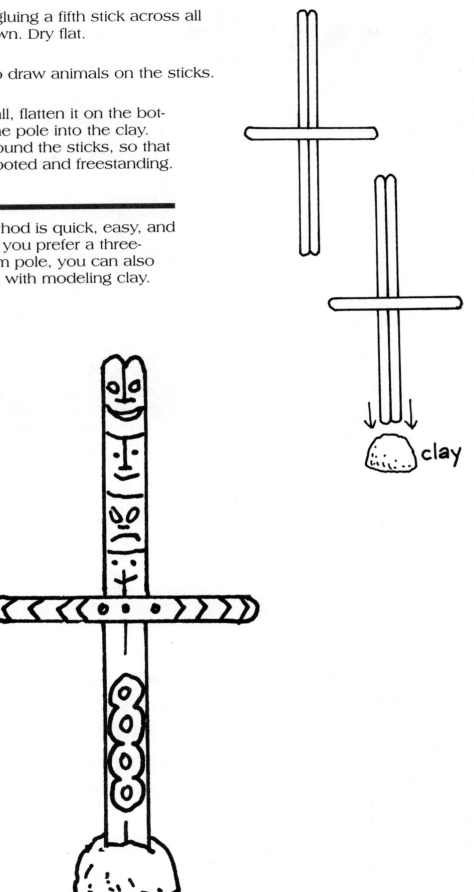

91

PLANK HOUSE

The Kwakiutl Indians traditionally lived along the Pacific coast just northeast of Vancouver Island in Victoria, Canada. In this lush environment, they had little difficulty obtaining the necessities of life. One of the greatest fishing grounds in the world, the cool, deep waters of the Northwest Coast provided them with a wide variety of food, while the region's tall trees offered all the materials they needed to make houses, clothing, fishing nets, baskets, and canoes.

Covered with long wooden planks, Kwakiutls' houses were built directly on the shore, with the ocean before them and the forest behind them. To protect the dwellings from tidal water, they were sometimes constructed on elevated platforms anchored on large poles and situated high atop mounds of earth or shell. Several families lived in each plank house, but partitions made from wood or woven cedar mats afforded each a measure of privacy. However, important families were far from shy about using their house's exterior to announce their status to their neighbors. Outside of the entrances to their homes, they erected totem poles, which featured carved images of people, animals, and spirits that could be read as stories about the family's wealth and power. Often the face of a mythical creature thought to be the family's ancestor was also painted on the planks surrounding the entrance, with the opening serving as the creature's mouth.

MATERIALS

popsicle sticks

glue, scissors

cardboard box
(8" x 8" or larger)

markers, paint

masking tape

2 twigs, toothpicks
cardboard (9" x 12")

small shells, pebbles,
sand

PROJECT ONE: PLANK HOUSE ON RAISED PLATFORM

DIRECTIONS

1. Line up 12 popsicle sticks vertically on a flat surface.

2. Spread glue on two sticks. Place one on the top and one of the bottom of the row of sticks as shown.

3. Repeat Steps 1 and 2 five more times. Allow the six sections to dry. These will be the walls and roof of your plank house.

4. Place the box upside down. Draw support poles at the corners and in the middle of all sides. Color them in. If desired, add a grainy and barklike texture to the surfaces.

5. Cut out the areas between the support poles.

6. Make a ladder to fit the height of your box. Place two twigs side by side, and tape them to the desk. Cut toothpicks to the appropriate size to form the rungs. Dab both ends of each toothpick with glue, and place them over the parallel sticks. Allow the ladder to dry.

7. Line up four of the popsicle stick sections, and tape them securely together. Apply tape horizontally across all four sections and vertically between each two.

8. Stand the four pieces up, bending them at the taped edges to form a box. The masking tape should be on the inside of the box and should not be visible from the outside.

9. Tape the untaped corner on the inside of the popsicle box.

10. Using the cardboard rectangle, create a base for the plank house. Color a portion of the rectangle with a blue marker to indicate water. Cover the rest of the cardboard with glue, and sprinkle it with sand.

11. Glue the bottom of the box's support poles to the sandy portion of the cardboard.

12. Glue pebbles and shells, here and there, on the sand.

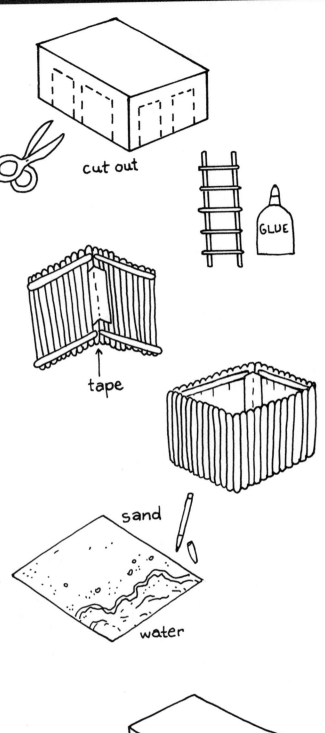

cut out

GLUE

tape

sand

water

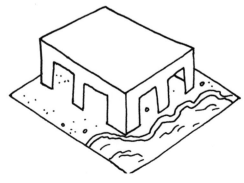

13. Place glue on the top of the horizontal popsicle stick of two opposite walls. Glue the two roof pieces to the top of walls, and bring them together at the top to form a gabled roof. Glue the roof pieces together, and allow them to dry.

14. Place the roof on its side and measure the triangle created on each side. Cut popsicle sticks to fit in this triangle, then glue them to the sides of the popsicle box. Allow to dry.

15. Place and glue roof to the popsicle box.

16. Use the black marker to indicate an entrance. (The entrance may be round or rectangular.)

17. Glue the bottom of the house to the platform. Dry.

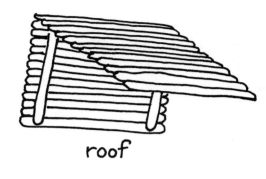

roof

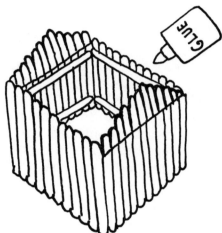

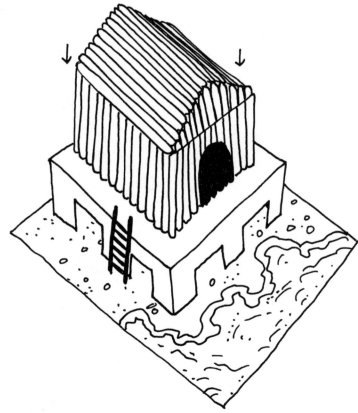

PLANK HOUSE WITH REMOVABLE ROOF

DIRECTIONS

1. Remove the shoe box lid, and draw a round or rectangular door on one end of the box. If you choose a round door, draw it slightly above the bottom of the box to create a raised threshold, and cut the circle out. If you choose a rectangular door, cut only on one side and across the top. Create a fold on the uncut side; the fold will act as a hinge for opening and shutting the door.

2. Cut a piece of cardboard to fit as a roof over your box. Fold this piece on its side and trace two triangular patterns as shown.

3. Cut and tape these triangular pieces to the sides of your roof.

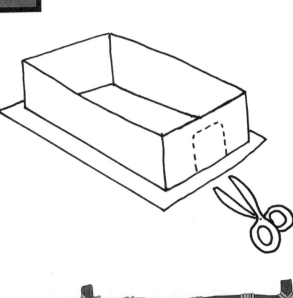

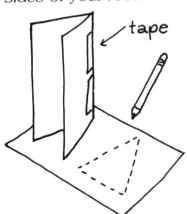

tape

4. Place the roof on to the box.

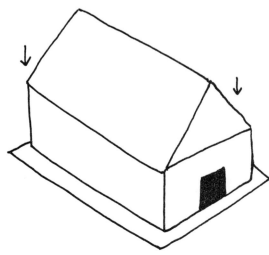

MATERIALS
shoe box
glue
pencil
scissors
cardboard
ruler
markers
brown paint
masking tape

5. Glue your model onto a cardboard base.

6. Paint the roof and base. You might want to remove the roof to complete this step. Allow to dry.

7. Use a ruler to measure and draw equally spaced lines on the model to indicate the planks. The planks on the sides of the house should go up and down. The planks on the roof should go across.

8. Color in the planks with markers.

TIP: A great resource for this project is *American Indian Habitats* by Nancy Simon and Evelyn Wolfson, pages 19–22.

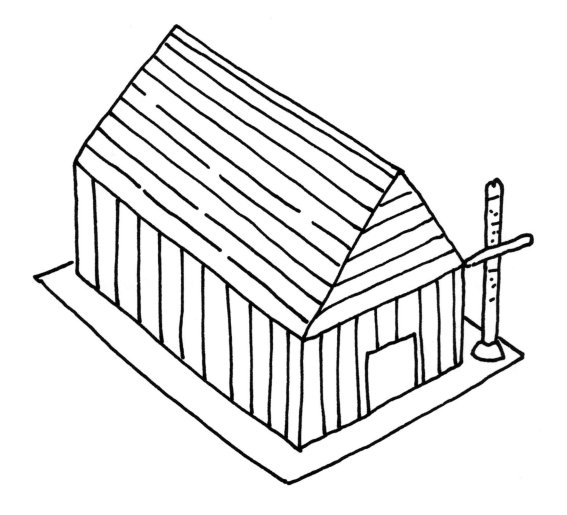

WHALE BUTTON BLANKET

Before they came in contact with non-Indians, Northwest Coast Indians made most of their clothing from cedar bark. By shredding the bark and weaving the strips together, they created tunics, skirts, and blankets, which they usually wore by wrapping them around their shoulders. These cedar bark garments were so tightly woven that they were nearly waterproof, a particularly important characteristic in the rainy Northwest.

In the early nineteenth century, England and American traders began setting up posts in the Northwest. In exchange for beaver furs, they offered the Indians an array of non-Indian trade goods, including black and dark blue blankets made of coarse woolen cloth. These trade blankets were not as water repellent as those the Indians made themselves, but they were easy to adorn using other items they obtained from the traders. Out of red cloth, Indian artisans made borders and animal-shaped appliques, which they sewed in the blankets' centers. Along the edges of the appliques, they sewed rows of tiny white buttons made from mother-of-pearl. "Button blankets" were often worn during ceremonies.

The project below is modeled after a modern button blanket made by a Kwatiutl artisan in 1974.

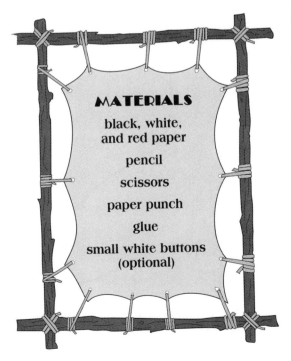

MATERIALS

black, white, and red paper

pencil

scissors

paper punch

glue

small white buttons (optional)

DIRECTIONS

1. Draw a whale—or use the pattern on the following page—and wavy lines (for waves) on black paper.

2. Cut it out, and punch holes (around the whale and wave edges).

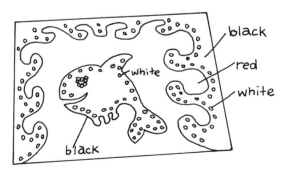

3. Make additional holes at the fins and the eye with the point of a pencil.

4. Glue the cutout on to white paper. The white background will appear through the holes and look like small white buttons.

5. Trim excess white paper around edges of the whale and waves.

6. Glue the whale and waves cutout on to red paper.

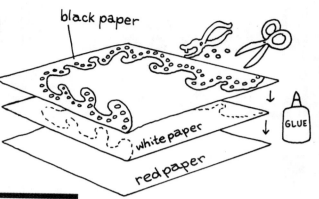

TIP: Use this technique to design your own button blankets featuring other animals revered by Northwest Coast Indians, such as the raven, eagle, and thunderbird.

KAYAK

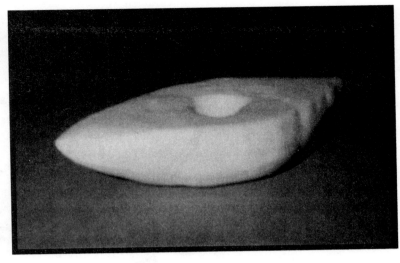

The Makah Indians inhabited a territory along Cape Flattery in what is now northwestern Washington State. Like most Indians of the region, the Pacific Ocean was their primary source for food. (In fact, their word for "food" and "fish" was the same.) In addition to being ingenious fishermen, the Makahs were also one of the few Northwest Coast tribes that hunted whales, an enterprise that required great skill and courage. To navigate the ocean waters while they pursued their prey, the Makahs built great dugout canoes and kayaks, large enough to carry both teams of hunters and their eighteen-foot-long harpoons.

DIRECTIONS

1. Make a shallow hole (about 1/4" deep) in the middle of the soap. (The diameter of the hole should be large enough to fit a clothespin.)

2. Remove the corners at the top of the boat by carving away tiny slivers of soap. (Students should be given ample time for this step, which should be done slowly and carefully.)

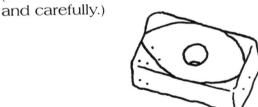

3. Remove the two remaining corners so that the kayak will be somewhat rounded on the bottom.

MATERIALS

Ivory soap bar

plastic knife

shortened clothespin

4. Place the clothespin figure in the hole on the top of the kayak. (In advance, the clothespin should be shortened by sawing or cutting the bottom off with garden clippers and smoothing the cut edges with sandpaper.)

TIPS:

1) Be sure to have a few extra bars of soap available, as some may break during the carving process. If possible, teachers should prepare several partially carved bars to give to children with broken bars so that they will not lag behind their classmates.

2) Very young children can draw a figure on oaktag to use in place of the clothespin. If using an oaktag figure, make a small slit in the soap instead of the hole described in Step 1.

3) Soap kayaks are significantly shorter and stouter than the Makah's carved wooden miniatures. Young children will be satisfied with these crude kayaks (and enjoy playing with them in the bathtub.) Older children, however, can use balsa wood to make a more realistic version. Balsa wood can be purchased in art stores, comes in various sizes, and is soft enough to carve easily.

Cedar-Bark Doll and Basket

Northwest Coast Indians made use of a wide variety of trees—including evergreens, spruce, fir, yew, and redwood—but the most versatile was the cedar. Its soft, even-grained wood easily could be broken into planks for building houses or carved into bowls, spoons, and tools. Its inner bark could be pounded into fibers as soft as cotton. Women twisted the fibers to form twine, which they wove to create baskets or intertwined with wool to make warm blankets and mats. Mats were often sewn into simple but comfortable shirts and skirts.

This project is based on a cedar-bark doll made by a Muckleshoot Indian in the 1700s.

DIRECTIONS

1. Draw a face and hair on the clothespin with a marker.

clothespin

2. Fold the fabric circles into quarters, and snip away 1/4" in the center.

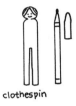

fabric

snip

feather

3. Place the circles flat on newspaper, and glue on blades of grass so that they radiate from the center. Dry.

4. Add pipe cleaner arms as directed in models. Also make a burden basket and another basket following the directions in models.

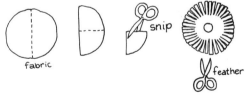

pipe cleaner

egg carton

basket

5. String some beads, and sew them to the top of the skirt so that the beads fall down.

6. Tape the shirt to the clothespin. Tape the cape above it.

MATERIALS
clothespin, markers

two fabric circles

scissors, newspaper

dry grass, glue

pipe cleaner

small beads

needle and thread

masking tape

apply shirt and skirt

optional basket

101

SEAL-SHAPED BOWL

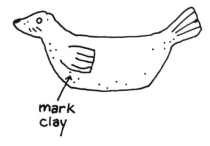

Many Indian groups of the Northwest Coast held grand feasts known as potlatches. These ceremonies were hosted by families seeking to impress their friends and neighbors with their generosity. In their world, a person obtained social status by giving away their wealth and possessions. Therefore, families used potlatches to compete with one another, each hoping to gain power in their village by setting out a meal more lavish and offering their guests gifts more valuable than those provided by any other potlatch hosts.

Much of the art made by Northwest Coast Indians was created to be used or given away during the potlatch. For instance, potlatch dishes often were held in beautifully carved wooden platters and bowls. Like fine china today, the bowls helped signal the importance of the event because they were only used for special occasions. Some serving bowls were decorated at the rim with inlaid shell; others were carved in the form of an animal, such as the seal-shaped bowl made by a Tlingit artist that inspired this project.

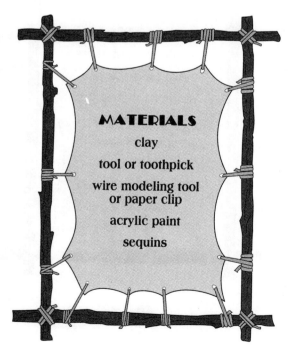

MATERIALS

clay

tool or toothpick

wire modeling tool or paper clip

acrylic paint

sequins

DIRECTIONS

1. From clay, model a seal with a flat bottom and upturned head and tail.

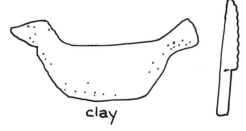

clay

2. Add on small balls of clay for the eyes, smoothing the clay completely around the edges.

mark clay

3. Use a pointed tool or toothpick to indicate mouth and fin lines.

4. Use a wire tool or paper clip to dig out a concave area in the seal's back if you want to use it as a container. The recessed area does not need to be large.

5. Paint the seal. Press sequins to the wet paint. (If thickly spread and moist, the paint will act as a glue.)

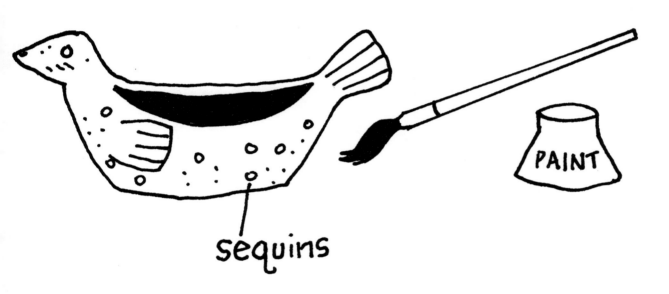

sequins

PAINT

TIP: Younger children can make this project as a sculpture or a paperweight. However, more advanced students will enjoy turning this piece into a container. (It makes an excellent desktop container for small objects, such as paper clips and tacks.)

ARCTIC

PREHISTORIC SCULPTURE

For many centuries, ivory from walrus tusks have been carved into simple, elegant forms by Inuit sculptors. Many prehistoric sculptures are engraved with patterns of dots, circles, and lines. Archaeologists can only speculate about the meanings these symbols might have had to the artists who drew them, although later Inuit art can provide some clues. For instance, one sculpture found on St. Lawrence Island and dating from A.D. 200–500 is incised with a series of small circles. The pattern is similar to designs on modern Inuit works that are meant to represent the underside of octopus tentacles.

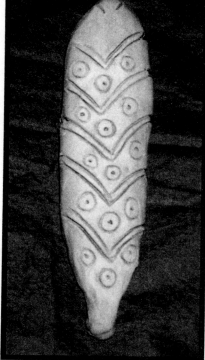

DIRECTIONS

1. Make an elongated, thick featherlike form of clay.

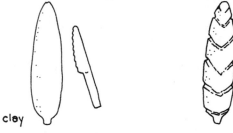

clay

2. Draw incised lines on it with a pointed tool.

3. Paint the clay form.

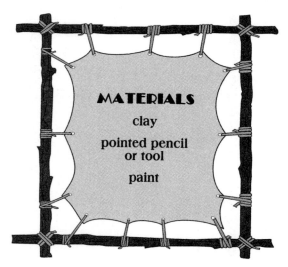

MATERIALS

clay

pointed pencil
or tool

paint

TIP: Suggest to students that they use the sculpture as a paperweight.

MASK

Living in a harsh Arctic climate, the Inuits had to struggle merely to survive from day to day. Perhaps to provide a release from the severity of their lives, humorous dances and songs were a part of many Inuit gatherings. Dancers often wore tattered clothing and face masks decorated with generous amounts of hair or fur as they performed their comic antics.

In the past, the Inuits carved these masks from wood, bone, or ivory. Since the early 1950s, however, many have been made from caribou skin using a technique that allows artists to make masks far more quickly. By this method, a wet caribou skin is stretched over a carved wooden form. As the skin dries, it retains the form's shape. Although the same form is used again and again, Inuit artists give each mask a unique look by adding tufts of fur for facial hair or bits of ivory for teeth.

DIRECTIONS

1. Cut an oval shape (slightly larger than your face) out of oaktag. Hold the oaktag up to your face, and mark where the eyeholes should be. Draw eye shapes around the marks, and cut out eyeholes.

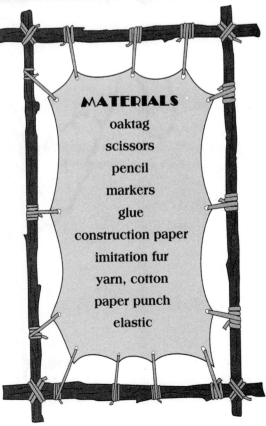

MATERIALS

oaktag

scissors

pencil

markers

glue

construction paper

imitation fur

yarn, cotton

paper punch

elastic

2. Draw other facial features.

3. If you would like to add a nose to your mask, make a cone out of construction paper. Cut several small slits at the bottom, and fold the resulting flaps toward the inside of the cone. Spread glue on the flaps, and attach the nose to the mask.

4. Glue on the fur, yarn, and/or cotton for hair, mustaches, eyebrows, and beards.

5. Punch a hole on each side of the mask, and tie on an elastic strap.

FINGER MASKS

During the Inuits' ceremonial dances, when men wore masks over their faces, women put on finger masks. Often carved from wood or stone and decorated with paint or caribou hair, these tiny masks were placed over several fingers, one mask on each hand. To the beat of a drum, the wearers then moved their hands slowly from side to side. After the late 1800s, finger masks were seldom used at ceremonials; today, any symbolic meanings they may have had have been forgotten.

DIRECTIONS

1. Draw two circles (large enough to fit your index and middle finger) near the bottom of the oaktag circle. (If you wish, use the template below instead.)

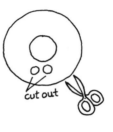

cut out

decorate

2. Draw a face at the center and color it in with markers.

3. Make multiple cuts around the face creating a feathered effect. (If you wish, glue feathers instead.)

feather

for fingers

4. Cut out the finger holes, and insert your fingers. Your finger mask is ready to use!

MATERIALS

oaktag circle
(4" diameter)

pencil

scissors

markers

glue (optional)

feathers (optional)

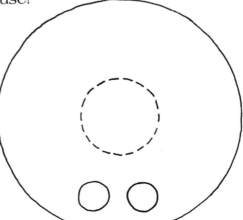

SNOW GOGGLES

While hunting on the frozen terrain in the harsh sun, Inuit men could easily become snow blind. To protect their eyes, they developed many types of goggles and eye shades. Most were carved out of wood or ivory (although in particularly frigid weather ivory goggles were not used because they could freeze to the wearer's face). The Inuits also made goggles out of sealskin, which they decorated with beads along the nosepiece.

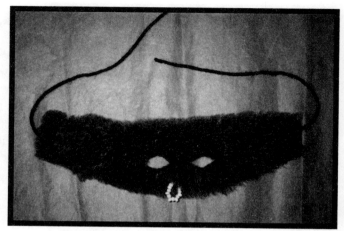

PROJECT ONE: IMITATION GOGGLES

DIRECTIONS

1. Cut two small holes at each end of the fur.

2. Cut two 6" pieces of yarn, and tie each throught the fur piece holes. (With younger children, you might suggest stapling the yarn to the fur instead.)

3. Place the fur piece over your eyes, so that the furry side is toward your face. Use a marker to indicate on the nonfurry side where the eyeholes should go. (You may suggest for students to work with partners in order to complete this step.)

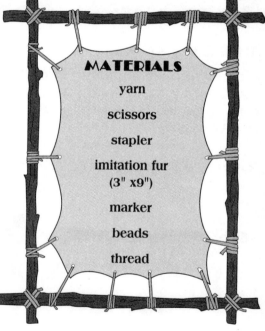

MATERIALS

yarn

scissors

stapler

imitation fur
(3" x9")

marker

beads

thread

4. Cut out the eyeholes.

5. String the beads, and sew them to nose area. Your goggles are ready to wear!

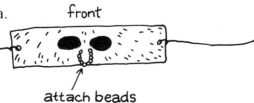

front

attach beads

PROJECT TWO: OAKTAG GOGGLES

MATERIALS

oaktag • pencil • scissors • marker • yarn • stapler

DIRECTIONS

1. Draw a masklike shape on oaktag, and cut it out.

2. Hold it up to your face, and use a marker to indicate where the eyeholes should go. (You may suggest that students work with partners to complete this step.)

3. Cut out thin eyeholes.

4. Using the marker, decorate the mask with lines.

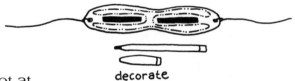

decorate

5. Cut two 6" lengths of yarn, and tie a knot at one end of each. Staple the knot of each yarn tie to each side of the mask's back.

CHILD DOLL

From the skins of the animals they hunted, Inuits made clothing that was ideal for their environment. Water-resistant seal-skins, used for summer clothing, protected them from seasonal rains. Thick and furry caribou skins, fashioned into parkas (hooded jackets), shielded them from the freezing winter. Parkas were designed to provide ease of movement while fitting snugly at the wrists, waist, and neck in order to hold in as much body heat as possible. For added comfort and warmth, the furry side of the skin was worn on the inside. In the winter, the Inuits also donned thick mittens and mukluks (woolen footwear), which they insulated with moss and down.

Inuit craftspeople made tiny versions of their own clothing to dress dolls they carved from ivory. Traditionally, fathers made these dolls as toys for their daughters. However, in recent decades, most dolls crafted by native artists have been made for sale.

PROJECT ONE: CLOTHESPIN DOLL

DIRECTIONS

1. Place the clothespin on paper, and draw the shape of a hooded parka around it. Make the parka fairly wide, so that after its sides are glued together, it still will be large enough to fit the clothespin figure. (Or use the pattern on the following page instead.)

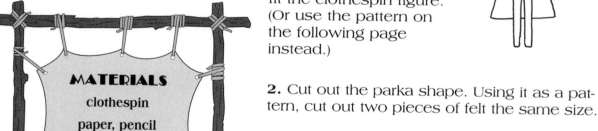

MATERIALS

clothespin

paper, pencil

scissors, felt

glue, marker

imitation fur
(optional)

black yarn
(optional)

2. Cut out the parka shape. Using it as a pattern, cut out two pieces of felt the same size.

3. Cut a circle (for the face) out of the hood of one felt piece.

for head

4. Cut out two pieces of felt in the shape of mittens. Glue the mittens to the inside edge of the sleeves of the felt piece with the hole in the hood.

5. Glue together the two parka pieces at the edges. Do not glue at the neck and at the bottom. Allow the glue to dry.

6. Wrap a piece of felt or fur around the lower section of the clothespin to make a skirt. Glue the skirt in place. If you prefer your doll to wear trousers, color its legs with a marker.

7. Slip the parka over the top of the clothespin.

8. Color on hair with a marker, or braid some yarn and glue it to the top of the clothespin.

braided yarn

9. Make sock-shaped mukluks from the felt, and glue them over the bottom of the clothespin.

PARKA TEMPLATE

CHIEF'S DAUGHTER DOLL

Traditionally, Inuit women wore jewelry they crafted from ivory, shell, and wood. But as shown in a 1793 painting of the daughter of Chief Kaigani of Dall Island, Alaska, after contact with non-Indians, wealthy women often preferred to adorn themselves with objects made from metal and trade goods obtained from foreign traders. The chief's daughter wears six bracelets and four anklets made of glowing copper—a metal precious to the Inuits, who thought it could bring health and well-being. Hanging around her neck is a silver fork, and her skirt is decorated with rows of buttons at the hem. She also wears a labret—a small plug placed through a slit cut in her flesh just below her lower lip. The Inuits believed that labrets greatly enhanced a woman's beauty.

DIRECTIONS

1. Draw a face and black hair on the top of the clothespin with markers.

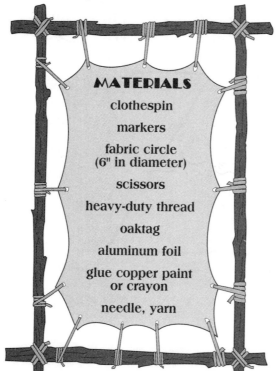

MATERIALS

clothespin

markers

fabric circle
(6" in diameter)

scissors

heavy-duty thread

oaktag

aluminum foil

glue copper paint
or crayon

needle, yarn

2. Draw rows of beads on the outside edge of the fabric circle.

3. Fold the circle in quarters, and cut a 1/4" hole in the center.

snip

4. Place the clothespin head through the hole. Tie the fabric around the doll's waist with heavy-duty thread or yarn to make a dress.

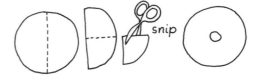

tie

5. Draw and cut out an oaktag fork pendant. Glue foil to it, and allow it to dry.

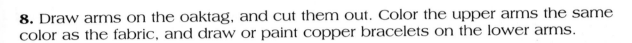
attach
necklace

6. Draw or paint copper anklets around the doll's lower legs.

7. Cut any excess foil from around the fork, and sew through the top with a needle and heavy thread. Knot the thread to make a necklace.

8. Draw arms on the oaktag, and cut them out. Color the upper arms the same color as the fabric, and draw or paint copper bracelets on the lower arms.

9. If desired, wrap a felt or fabric scrap around the doll's shoulders to make a cape.

10. Glue on yarn hair.

PROJECT TWO: CLAY DOLL
MATERIALS

clay• oaktag circle (1" in diameter) • black marker • 3 pom-poms (one 1 1/2" and two 1/2" in diameter) • glue

DIRECTIONS

1. Make a clay body, approximately 2" tall. Allow the clay to dry.

clay

2. Draw a face on the oaktag circle.

3. Apply glue to the large pom-pom, and attach the face.

apply
to
pom-pom

4. Apply glue to the bottom of the pom-pom, and attach it to the top of the clay body. Hold glued pieces in place until they are secure.

5. Glue the small pom-poms to the ends of the hands to create fur mittens for the doll.

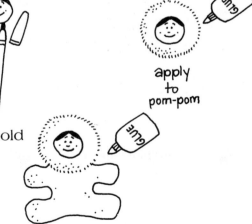

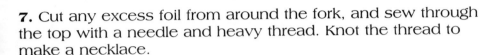

115

Toy Top

In the Arctic homeland of the Inuits, the sun shines only a few hours daily in the winter. To pass the time and lighten their moods during these long, dark days, adults and children alike loved to play games. Many of the favorites among youngsters involved a simple top, which they made themselves from clay and a stick. When children wanted to create a special top, they used paint and feathers as decorations.

MATERIALS

clay

half popsicle stick

feather

markers

DIRECTIONS

1. Make a clay ball, and flatten one side. Mold a tapering round bottom on the other side.

2. Insert the broken end of the stick and the feather into the center of the flattened side. Allow the clay to dry.

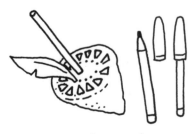

add stick and feather

decorate

3. Draw designs on the side of the top with markers.

4. Ask children to create their own top game!

TIP:

Use the top as a spinning device!

SNOW GEESE SCULPTURE

White snow geese are native to the Arctic, although they migrate to northern regions of the United States in winter. The beauty of these birds inspired an Inuit artist of King Island, Alaska, to create the white bent wood sculpture on which the project below is based. Made in 1990, the sculpture began as a flat piece of wood, on which the artist sketched the image of several geese. The sculptor then skillfully cut away the background area and steamed the wood, causing the birds' wings to curl forward.

DIRECTIONS

1. Draw a line about 1" to 2" from the bottom of the paper to form a border.

2. Lightly sketch two geese in pencil. With a black marker, outline the sketch and draw the birds' eyes. (If you wish, use the template on page 118.)

3. Cut out background areas.

MATERIALS

white paper
(12" x 18")

pencil

black marker

scissors

glue

4. Overlap the border and part of the wings and glue them together to form a circular sculpture.

TIP: For a sturdier sculpture, use a piece of oaktag with white paper glued to each side. Be sure to glue the paper to the oaktag in advance.

117

STENCIL PRINT

The Inuits living in the community of Cape Dorset in Canada have become well-known for their printmaking—an art form they learned from non-Indian teachers in the 1950s. Their prints, which are made primarily for sale, are now popular with collectors from around the world.

The Cape Dorset Inuits often use stencils to make their prints. With this technique, holes are cut into a piece of oaktag or plastic to create a design. Then paint or ink is spread or sprayed across the stencil and seeps through the holes onto a piece of paper positioned below.

DIRECTIONS

1. Draw a bird image on a piece of oaktag.

2. Cut out the drawing, so the background remains in one piece. The image will be a hole in the middle of the oaktag.

3. Place the oaktag stencil over a piece of paper.

4. Dab the sponge into the paint, and test by dabbing it on newspaper to achieve an even covering of paint.

5. Dab the paint sponge over the holes in the stencil. Remove the stencil, and allow the print to dry.

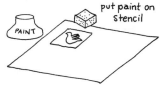

put paint on stencil

PAINT

6. Add white dots for the birds' eyes.

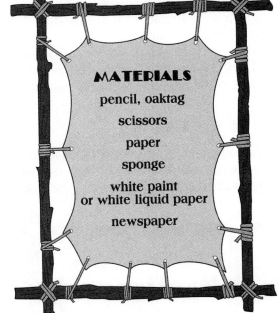

MATERIALS

pencil, oaktag

scissors

paper

sponge

white paint
or white liquid paper

newspaper

TIP: A stencil print is similar to a silhouette. You can achieve a similar design effect by cutting birds out of black paper and gluing them to a white background. Eyes can be made with paper punch.

WALL HANGING

Traditionally, Inuit women had to be accomplished seamstresses in order to fashion the warm fur parkas their families needed to protect themselves from the Arctic cold. Now able to buy much of their clothing, many Inuit women of Quebec, Canada, today devote their practical sewing skills to the purely creative task of making decorative wall hangings. By cutting out cloth appliqués and stitching them to a black background, these artists seem to paint with fabric. Their lively, colorful creations illustrate scenes of traditional life, featuring Inuits hunting, cooking, and making tools. Appliqués of animals, sometimes dressed playfully in human clothing, often are sprinkled through the composition or positioned along the sides to form a border. The inspiration for the project below is a wall hanging crafted in 1990 on which figures of seals and whales appear to swim around the edges of the work.

DIRECTIONS

1. On paper, sketch arctic animals, such as whales, seals, bears, and birds. Concentrate on the outline of each animal. Because these sketches will be used as patterns, no details are needed. (Try using the templates on the following page.)

MATERIALS

paper

pencil

fabric-cutting scissors

pins

felt of different colors (including black)

needle and thread or glue

2. Cut out the animal patterns.

3. Pin the patterns to the felt, and cut them out. The same sketch may be reused several times. Try cutting the same animal shape out of different colors.

4. Stitch or glue the animals to a piece of black felt. If you are sewing, add details with stitches. If you are gluing, add details with small pieces of different colors of felt.

Mesoamerica
Central America
South America

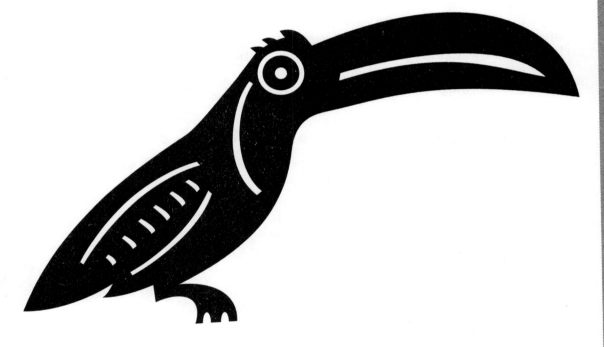

MOLAS

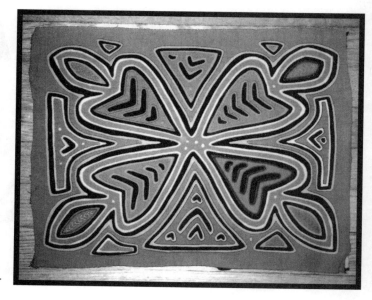

The San Blas Islands off the coast of Panama are home to the Cunas, who have been making appliquéd fabric panels known as molas since the fifteenth century. Molas are made from many layers of brightly colored fabric on which various shapes are sewn or cut out to reveal the color of the cloth beneath. For more than 100 years, the Cunas have used molas to decorate blouses and other clothing, although today many non-Indians buy Cuna molas to display as wall hangings.

Many of the colorful patterns found on molas are derived from designs associated with the Cunas' centuries-old custom of body painting. Featured in these designs are geometric shapes, plants, animals, and mythological beings. In recent years, however, the Cunas' increased contact with other peoples has led them to develop new types of designs. Molas now are likely to include figures of political and sports personalities as well as images the Cunas have seen in magazines and books.

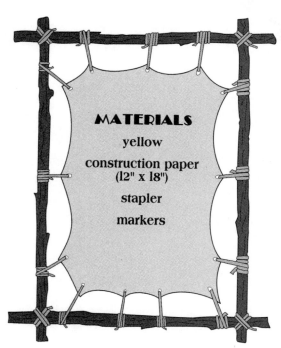

MATERIALS

yellow

construction paper
(l2" x l8")

stapler

markers

PROJECT ONE:
MOLA PENCIL CASE
DIRECTIONS

l. Fold a sheet of paper four times. Unfold and create a symmetrical design.

2. Gllue yarn along the lines of your design.

3. Use a marker of another color to fill in the background with thick lines.

add yarn

decorate

PROJECT TWO: MOLA FELT PURSE

MATERIALS

felt rectangle • scraps of felt in various colors • needle and thread (or glue) • pins • scissors

DIRECTIONS

1. Fold up the bottom third of the felt rectangle, and sew the sides together. Fold down the top third to form a flap.

2. Cut out a simple animal, fish, or geometric shape from a felt scrap.

3. Cut slits in the shape. Place a felt scrap of a contrasting color on the back of the shape so that the color can be seen through all the slits.

4. Pin both felt pieces to the flap. Sew (or glue) around the edges.

5. Cut out lines of felt. Pin them to the background and then sew (or glue) them to the flap with a single line of stitches down the middle of each piece.

PROJECT THREE: MOLA ARM BAND

MATERIALS

felt • glue • rickrack • stapler • yarn

DIRECTIONS

1. Cut a rectangle of felt that fits around your arm.

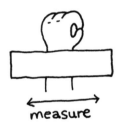

measure

2. Glue rickrack along the center of the felt piece. Allow the glue to dry.

decorate

3. Staple a yarn tie to each end.

125

ALPACA FIGURINE

The Incas were highly skilled at working with gold, silver, and copper. They poured the molten metals into molds, and once they had cooled, soldered these molded pieces together to create tiny, delicate sculptures, often of animals. Favorite subjects included the llama and the wooly alpaca, which the Incas domesticated and valued greatly as pack animals.

DIRECTIONS

1. Place the cylinder on oaktag, and trace around it to roughly form the shape of an alpaca's body. Remove the cylinder, and add two legs, a neck, and a head with ears to finish the drawing of the alpaca. (Use the template on the following page, if necessary.)

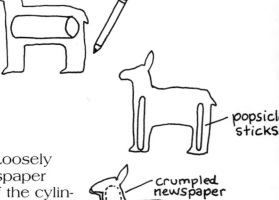

popsicle sticks

2. Cut out two oaktag alpacas. Tape popsicle sticks behind the legs and necks for added strength.

3. Tape the alpacas to the sides of the cylinder. Loosely tape the necks together, and stuff crumpled newspaper inside to make the neck thicker and sturdier. Stuff the cylinder with newspaper as well.

crumpled newspaper

tape

MATERIALS

4" cardboard cylinder

oaktag

black marker

masking tape

popsicle sticks

newspaper

gray yarn

scissors

silver paint, glue

4. Make a yarn tail, and tape it in place. Cover the entire sculpture (except for the tail) with masking tape.

5. Paint the sculpture silver, and allow it to dry. Glue gray yarn to the back so it hangs down on both sides.

yarn

cover with tape

paint

MOSAIC MASK

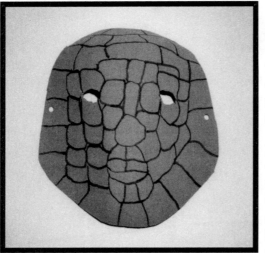

Perhaps the greatest pre-Columbian Indian civilization was that of the Mayas. These peoples built large urban centers and massive buildings, invented a complex writing system, and created much of the most beautiful artwork of the ancient world.

Most Maya art was made to glorify their kings. Many surviving works were buried with these rulers in colossal tombs. Among these burial offerings were mosiac masks, which were placed over the faces of the corpses. These masks were covered with hundreds of pieces of colored stone—most often turquoise or green jade, which was a symbol of wealth and power among the Mayas. On many masks, facial details were formed from other materials. Shells often were used for teeth and the whites of the eyes; obsidian, for the eyes' pupils; and pyrite, for the lips.

DIRECTIONS

1. Using sharp scissors, cut out the rounded side of the container in the shape of a mask. Avoid cutting too near the container's bottom where the plastic is especially thick.

2. Hold the mask to your face, and draw eye shapes with a marker. (Classmates may prefer to do this step with partners, one student drawing the eyes as the other holds up his or her mask.) Cut out the eye openings.

MATERIALS

large plastic milk or water container

scissors

black marker

oaktag

turquoise paint

paper punch

elastic

3. Cut a piece of oaktag the same size as your mask and tape or glue over the plastic.

4. Paint the mask turquoise. Allow the paint to dry.

5. Draw lines (with marker) to mimic the shapes of turquoise stones.

6. Punch a hole on each side and tie a piece of elastic across the back. Your mask is ready to wear!

tape oaktag onto plastic

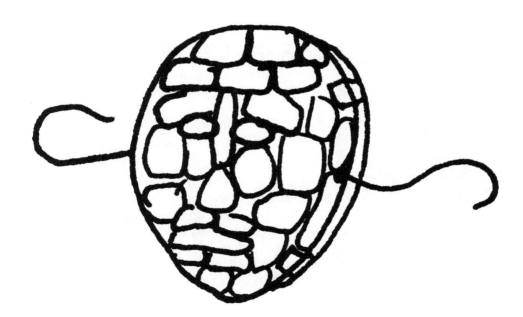

TEMPLE AT CHICHEN ITZA

The Toltec peoples came to power in Mesoamerica in the late a.d. 900s. Using only stone tools, the Toltecs constructed massive temples that were so sturdy that some still stand. One of the most impressive was built in the city of Chichen Itzá. This great structure was probably built to house the burial chamber of a Toltec king.

The base of the pyramid-shaped temple measures 179 square feet. On each side of the four sides of the temple is a staircase of 91 steps. Today, the temple is a popular destination for fitness-conscious tourists from around the world, who want to climb to the top of the grand temple just as the Toltecs did 1,000 years ago.

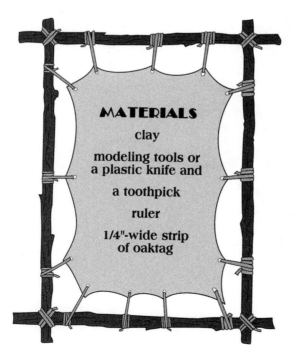

MATERIALS

clay

modeling tools or
a plastic knife and

a toothpick

ruler

1/4"-wide strip
of oaktag

DIRECTIONS

1. Make a 1" square cube of clay. Spread it on a flat surface to form a slab about 1/4" thick.

2. Place the clay cube on top of the slab, and cut the slab to make a square base about 1 1/2" on each side. When cutting, use the 1/4"-inch oaktag strip as a measuring tool: just place it along each side of the cube, and cut along the strip's outside edge.

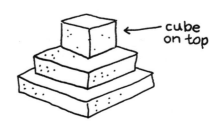

cube on top

3. Make another slab of clay, and place the first slab and the cube on top of it. Trim the second slab, so that it protrudes 1/4" beyond the first. (Again, for easy measuring, place the oaktag strip along each side of the first slab, then cut along the outside edge.)

4. Repeat Step 4 seven more times. (Your model should then have nine trimmed slabs topped by a cube.)

5. Make four rectangular clay slabs for the sides. These slabs will be the temple's staircases. With a pointed tool, draw a line along each of the long sides of the slabs. Draw multiple lines across the slabs to represent stairs.

6. Place one slab vertically down the middle of each side of the temple.

7. Add details to the cube at the top of the structure by attaching bits of small clay or making tiny indentions into its sides.

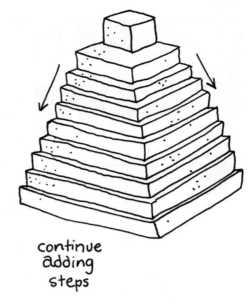

continue
adding
steps

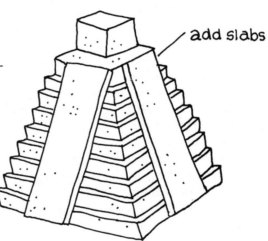

add slabs

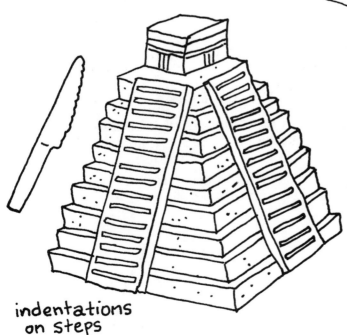

indentations
on steps

BEADED NECKLACE

The Yanomamos live in scattered farming villages in the Amazon River Basin on the border between Venezuela and Brazil. Their territory is so isolated that, until recent years when anthropologists began studying the tribe, the Yanomamos had had almost no contact with other peoples. Although today their exposure to the outside world is ever increasing, they actively resist its influences as much as possible. Now numbering more than 20,000, the Yanomamos prefer to live much as their ancestors always have in their remote jungle homeland.

Among the most important traditions still observed by the Yanomamos are their ceremonial feasts. At these celebrations, the tribespeople enjoy eating sumptuous food, performing dances, and parading proudly before one another wearing decorative body paint and fine ornaments, including long strands of beads. When these ceremonial bead strings are laid flat, they look like a figure 8. When worn, the smaller circle goes around the neck, the larger circle goes around the body, and beaded strings cross over the chest. On some occasions, the Yanomamos wear two strands at once.

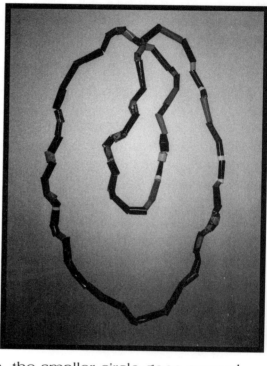

MATERIALS

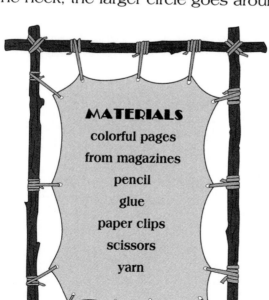

colorful pages from magazines

pencil

glue

paper clips

scissors

yarn

DIRECTIONS

1. Cut triangles out of magazine pages.

2. Using a pencil, roll each triangle into small cylinders.

3. Apply glue to the tip of each triangle. Allow glue to dry.

4. String beads on a long piece of yarn. Your beaded necklace is ready to wear!

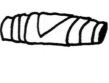

TIP: Pages from *National Geographic* magazine are excellent for beadmaking. In addition to being colorful, they are printed on heavy paper. To avoid wasting classroom time flipping through magazines, select the pages you want to use before beginning this project.

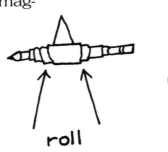

roll

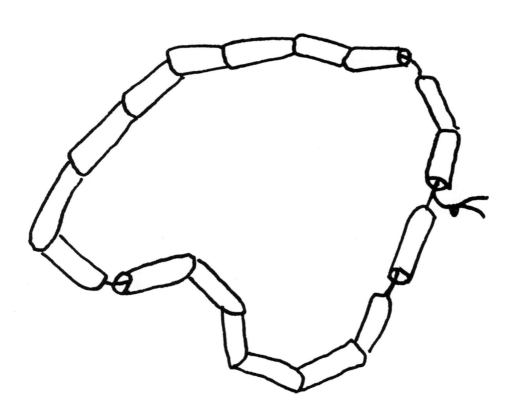

METHODS AND MATERIALS

Below are methods and materials frequently called for in the projects in this book. Included also are suggestions for how they can be used most effectively. At the end of this section, I also have noted some tips for proper preparation and clean up.

GLUE

White liquid glue is superior to paste, especially when joining materials other than paper.

White glues dry clear, so they can be used as a protective sealing coat over paint. A coat of glue will also act as a binder on a smooth surface, allowing paint to adhere more permanently. Paint will also cover more surfaces if it is mixed with thinned white glue; if a large amount of thinned glue is added, the paint's color will be more transparent.

For tricky gluing situations, thicken white glue by placing it in a freezer for a few hours. The cooled glue will bond to surfaces more readily. However, be careful not to leave it in too long or it will freeze.

Be careful to use the correct amount of glue. A thin coating of glue spread over a surface will dry more quickly. If you apply too much glue, it will escape out the edges. Equally important, keep glued objects still until the glue begins to set. Paper clips, elastic, masking tape, or pinch clothespins can be used to hold the objects in place temporarily.

For difficult jobs, apply gentle pressure while waiting for the glue to dry.

When gluing objects together, always let gravity help you. If you need to place glue on the side of an object, move the object if possible so the side to take the glue is on top.

When gluing a fluffy object to a surface, apply the glue on the fluffy object, rather than the surface to which it will be attached.

MASKING TAPE

Masking tape can be used to cover a construction instead of papier mâché. The tape can then be colored with acrylic paint or with the ink from permanent markers. (If the construction is painted with glue first, it will be sturdier and the tape will not dry out and lift as readily.) Tape can also be used to cover a slippery surface that otherwise would not take paint easily.

If a thin surface, such as cardboard or oaktag, is to be papier mâche'd, covering the surface with masking tape first will prevent it from becoming limp.

PAPIER MACHE

Papier mâché is a wonderfully versatile material. Using papier mâché, you can make large objects that will not break easily.

If possible, use wheat paste (also called wallpaper paste) for papier mâché. It is readily available and inexpensive. (In a pinch, flour and water may be used instead, but because it is more difficult to mix, it is often lumpy.) When mixing wheat paste, make it on the thick side; if it is too thin, it is likely to drip. Store the paste in closed plastic containers.

When papier mâchéing, give children their own containers of paste. Students are apt to become so involved in their papier mâchéing that they inadvertently drip the paste. Having individual containers helps point out who is responsible and, therefore, who should clean up any dripping.

Instruct students to work closely over their paste container. They should be told to use their thumb and forefinger to apply paste to the paper and to remove extra paste, returning any excess to the container.

Work over many layers of newspaper. If the top newspaper becomes moist, students can begin using it on their construction. In addition to keeping the classroom neat, this simple rule saves time and paste.

CLAY

Clay is probably the best material for making three-dimensional objects. Many schools keep clay on hand as a regular supply, but if yours does not, it is worth ordering it specially. Keep in mind that a little can go a long way. Students do not need to make large objects; in fact, small amounts of clay are easier to work with.

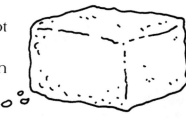

Give students their supply of clay on a Styrofoam tray. The tray can be used to hold their finished work, thus minimizing the chance that the projects will break as they are moved. Instruct students to put their initials on their trays so that ownership is never in question.

Rough edges on clay objects can be smoothed with a little water, but objects should first be fully molded. If students smooth their work with water too soon, the clay can become overly soft and limp.

If your supply of clay becomes too dry and stiff, simply add a little water or a wet sponge inside a plastic bag. Knead the bag to ensure an even consistency. (Be sure to tell students that if they break an unfired clay object at home, they can use the same method to recycle the clay.)

Always work with clay over newspaper. When students are finished, the edges should be gathered carefully to enclose any small bits of clay for conveyance to the trash basket.

If you cannot purchase clay, you can make a claylike material from baking soda, cornstarch, and water using the recipe below.

BASIC WHITE CLAY RECIPE

Materials

2 cups of baking soda (l pound package} • l cup of cornstarch • l 1/4 cups of cold water • plate 8 damp cloth

1. Mix together baking soda and corn starch in a saucepan.
2. Add water and cook over medium heat, stirring constantly. When the mixture is the consistency of moist mashed potatoes, turn it out on a plate. Cover the plate with a damp cloth to prevent the clay from drying prematurely.
3. When cool enough to handle, knead the clay like dough. The clay is then ready to mold.
4. Store any extra clay in a tightly closed plastic bag in the refrigerator for later use.

Food coloring can be added to the clay while it is still wet. With a little kneading, it will blend in easily, giving the clay a nice pastel color. When dry, objects made from either plain white or colored clay can be decorated with markers or paint.

This clay also can be spread on a flat surface and cut with cookie cutters. Although not as creative as making one's own shapes, using cutters is often enjoyed by students. Cookie-cutter shapes can be used with other small sculptures for creative play.

You may want to make copies of this recipe to send home with your students. Parents will appreciate having it on hand for rainy days.

PAPER SCULPTURE

Making sculptures from paper is easy, inexpensive, and quick. In addition, making small paper models is a convenient way of experimenting with an idea for a sculpture that you later intend to make using a more substantial material.

ACRYLIC PAINT

Acrylic paint is water based, hence free of fumes and easy to clean up, but it is just as durable as an oil-base paint. Acrylic's durability particularly makes it the paint of choice for constructions. A coat of acrylic paint will strengthen a construction and make it so resistant to moisture that it can be dusted with a damp cloth. Acrylic paint also can to cover a wide variety of surfaces. It will cling permanently to most objects without cracking.

Store acrylic paint in a container with a fairly wide mouth. Plastic jars are best, but glass containers are acceptable since students rarely drop paint jars. Be sure that your brushes are not too tall for the containers, or their long handles may get in students' way.

SCISSORS

For most classroom activities, student scissors, even with blunt ends, are adequate. However, keep a pair of large scissors available for teacher use.

Advise students to use the joint of the scissor blades rather than the blades' points to cut. (Students can cut nearly every material if they follow this simple rule.) Also, teach them to hold limp materials, such as yarn, taut when cutting them.

BEADS

Buying beads may be a little expensive, but even a few beads can add sparkle to a project. They are also among children's favorite art supplies.

If beads are not in your budget, they can be made out of clay. (Students will enjoy molding clay beads occasionally, but do not make it a regular activity because it can quickly become tiresome.) Even young children can make beads by cutting drinking straws into small sections. This method is quick, easy, and inexpensive, and good to keep in mind for projects that require a large number of beads. Macaroni also can be used as a bead substitute.

You can also recycle beads from used items. For instance, old beaded car seats or costume jewelry are great sources of beads. Ask parents for any such items they are discarding or visit yard sales to buy them cheaply.

Old wooden beads are easy to paint if you first place them on a stick or a small dowel. For drying, put the other end of the stick into a cardboard box so that the stick stands upright.

SMOCKS

Students should wear smocks for most art projects. They may resist putting them on unless the teacher also wears one, which I recommend for even the neatest adults.

An old oversize shirt with the sleeves cut off at the elbow makes a good smock. Before working, the sleeves should be rolled up; it is easier to wash arms than sleeves!

Even when wearing a smock, students can get art materials on their clothing. If they do, act quickly. First, remove as much of the unwanted substance as possible with a dry towel. Then wash the area with soap and water. Even if you do not get the spot out entirely, a presoaking and machine wash will probably do the rest.

GATHERING MATERIALS

Acquiring all the materials for a project can take a little time and organization. Make your job easier by telling friends and relatives about your needs; most people are receptive and eager to contribute. Also, be sure to send a list home with your students. Sometimes a parent will know of a wonderful source of certain materials of which you were unaware.

Fellow teachers can be drafted for the cause as well. Post a note listing the materials you need by a copy machine or on the school refrigerator. To encourage their help, set out a labeled container, in which they can leave the items.

Requesting recycled materials from students has several added benefits. It gets them involved in a project early on, which is always desirable, and provides a lesson in recycling. Encourage students, if possible, to bring in enough supplies for several children. You will gather materials more quickly, and your helpers will feel good about their extra effort.

If you are relying on others to bring in supplies for a specific project, do not schedule the activity until the all of the needed materials are in your classroom. People who promise to provide supplies, no matter how well-intentioned, are likely to forget sometimes.

CLEANUP

Always keep in mind that the cleaner you work, the less there will be to clean up at the end.

Make students responsible for cleaning their own areas. Those who finish first should help others. Along with the satisfaction they get from doing something for someone else, they should also be given an assurance that someday the students they help will return the favor.

For projects that involve painting, students should bring their paint containers and brushes to a paint table as their first step in cleaning up. (Making this the priority will help avoid countless accidents.) Next, students should take their artwork to a drying area, then discard any newspaper that has been spread on the floor to catch drips and finally wash their hands.

While students are washing up, gather the paintbrushes in a container of water and leave them to soak. When the sink is free, begin cleaning them, first removing most of the paint by swooshing them in water and then washing them with soap. (If you inadvertently allow paint to dry on your brushes, soaking and soaping still might revitalize them.) In order to keep brushes pliable, be sure to remove all paint in the bristles. Store brushes in a container with the bristles up so they keep their shape.

BIBLIOGRAPHY

American Indian Tools and Ornaments by Evelyn Wolfson (David McKay, 1981)

Arts of the Indian America by Jamake Highwater (Harper and Row, 1983)

The American Indian by Oliver La Farge (Western Publishing, 1974)

Arts of the Raven by W. Bill Duff (Vancouver Art Gallery, 1974)

Authentic Indian Designs by Maria Naylor (Dover, 1975)

Crafts of Many Cultures by Aurelia Gomez (Scholastic, 1992)

Ethnic and Tourist Arts by Nelson Graburn (University of California Press, 1976)

Explorations by D. G. Noble (School of American Research Press, 1984)

Growing up Indian by Evelyn Wolfson (Walker and Company, 1986)

Inub, Bering Sea by William Fitzhugh (Smithsonian Institute Press, 1982)

Language and Art in the Navajo Universe by Gary Witherspoon, (University of Michigan Press, 1977)

Molas: Folk Art of the Cuna Indians by Ann Parker (Barre Publishers, 1977)

Native American Art in Evolution by Edwin Wade (Hudson Press, 1986)

Native American Heritage by Evan Maurer (Art Institute of Chicago, 1977)

Native Americans by Flights of Fancy (Scholastic, 1991)

Native Americans by Westhorp (Crescent, 1993)

Native Arts of North America by Christian Feest (Oxford University Press, 1980)

Native Arts of North America by George Corbin (Harper and Row, 1988)

North American Indian Mythology by Cottie Burland (Peter Bedrick Books, 1986)

Pre-Columbian Art by Ferdinand Anton (Harry N. Abrams, Inc., 1968)

Southwest Indian Tribes by Tom Bahti (K. C. Publications, 1969)

Yanomamo by Napoleon A. Chagnon (Holt, Rinehart and Watson, Inc., 1968)

Zuni Fetishes by Frank Hamilton Cushing (K. C. Publications, 1990)

NOTES